A carriage approaching St Mark's in 1873

A HISTORY OF ST MARK'S

CHURCH LIFE IN BROOMHILL AND

BROOMHALL, SHEFFIELD

EDITED BY DAVID PRICE

ST MARK'S CHURCH,
BROOMHILL AND BROOMHALL,
SHEFFIELD

Printed by:
ALD Design and Print
279 Sharrow Vale Road
Sheffield S11 8ZF
Telephone: 0114 267 9402
Email: a.lofthouse@btinternet.com

ISBN 978-1-901587-99-9

CONTENTS

LIST OF ILLUSTRATIONS

CONTRIBUTORS

The preparation of this book has been a team effort by the following people, almost all drawn from St Mark's congregation:

- **Michael Hunt.** Author of Chapter 8. Former university lecturer. Editor or author of several academic books and articles. Church Warden of St Mark's since 2011.
- **Helen Mathers.** Author of Chapter 2. Historian. Author of *Steel City Scholars, the Centenary History of the University of Sheffield* (James and James, 2005).
- **Sarah Moore.** Glossary and marketing. MA in Historical Research. Has developed resources and workshops around topics including analysis in assessment for social workers. Has taught in the UK and Middle East.
- **Tim Moore.** Author of Chapters 3 and 4. MA in English Literature from Sheffield University. Has written book reviews and blogs, as well as numerous short stories and a novel, under the name Richard McCarthy.
- **David Price.** Editor and author of Chapters 5, 6 and 7. Former civil servant. Church Warden of St Mark's 1999-2003. Author of *Sheffield Troublemakers: Rebels and Radicals in Sheffield History* (Phillimore, 2008).
- **Rosie Richards.** Author of Chapter 1. Former social worker. Author of *The Parish Church of St Mary the Virgin, Beighton* (1991). Contributed to local history projects in Eckington, Norton and Beighton.
- **John Roach.** Glossary and Index. Professor Emeritus of Education, University of Sheffield. Author of books and articles on the history of education and local history.
- **Carol Rowe.** Copy-editor. Freelance copy-editor of academic books and journals and translator of, among other things, *Western Muslims and the Future of Islam*, by Tariq Ramadan (OUP, 2004).
- **Richard Taylor.** Author of Chapter 9. Author of *How to Read A Church* (Rider, 2003) and writer and presenter of BBC television's *Churches: How To Read Them*, *A Short History of Bells* and *Pugin: God's Own Architect*.
- **Revd Dr Ian Wallis.** Author of Chapter 10. Vicar of St Mark's since 2009. Former Principal of the Northern Ordination Course. Author of *Holy Saturday: Rediscovering the Legacy of Jesus* (SPCK, 2000).
- **John Whitmill.** Research, particularly for Chapter 2. Graduate in Theology and Religious Studies at York St John University. Works at University of Sheffield Library.

History team: Front row from left: Tim Moore, Sarah Moore, Helen Mathers, John Roach, Michael Hunt. Rear row: Rosie Richards, David Price, Carol Rowe, Ian Wallis

Richard Taylor   John Whitmill

ACKNOWLEDGEMENTS

In preparing this book for publication we have received a great deal of help from a wide variety of people – mainly individuals associated with St Mark's but also more widely. We thank them all and apologise to any whose names do not appear below. Any mistakes or omissions should be attributed to the authors.

We are indebted to the Rt Revd Steven Croft, Bishop of Sheffield, for his encouragement and to the Sheffield Church Burgesses Trust, Patrons of St Mark's, for their financial support.

We are most grateful to David Bradley for all the work and skill that went into the maps and plans he has provided for this book. We owe a debt to Ordnance Survey in preparing the map of parish boundaries, which contains public sector information licensed under the Open Government Licence v 1.0 courtesy of the Open Data provisions. Similarly, we greatly appreciate Kay Aitch's artist's impressions of the iron church and the reredos and pulpit of the 1871 stone church.

We thank the staff of Sheffield Local Studies Library and Sheffield City Archives for their help with records, maps and illustrations. More generally, we appreciate the care that the City Archives take in looking after our church records. We are also grateful for help from the staff at Bishopscroft, Sheffield, Sheffield Diocesan Office, Sheffield Diocesan Registry, the statistician of the Archbishop's Council, the Borthwick Institute in York and the Library of the Institution of Civil Engineers in London.

Among many individual helpers, we would mention the Rt Revd Michael Adie, the Revd Adrian Alker and Christine Alker, Dr Roy Barry and Beryl Barry, the Revd Dr Michael Bayley and Fleur Bayley, Eileen Beech, Stuart Bennett, the Revd Jane Bolton, Andrew Braybrook and Margaret Braybrook (nee Wardlow), Pam Broadhurst, Anne and Arthur Button, Christine Chambers, Pat Collins, Janet Earwaker, Pauline Elliott, the Revd John Giles, Roy Godden, the Revd Sue Hobley, the Revd Dr Noel Irwin, the Revd Nick Jowett, Ann Lewin, Dr Margaret Lyons, Professor David McClean, Anne Padget, Jane Padget, the Revd Michael Paton, Peter Pace, David Ryder, Peter Ryder, Ann Sapcote, Robin and Eve Saunders, the Revd John Simmonds, Donald and Josie Smith, Samuel Taylor, John Trigg, Maureen Whitebrook, Peter Whitmill, Eva Wilkinson and Dr Nyra Wilson. Michael Hunt is most grateful to those members of the congregation whose thoughtful comments in a 2012 survey helped to inform his chapter.

We are most grateful to the following owners, trustees of copyright and holders of collections for their permission to publish these images: Sheffield Local Studies Library (and the *Picture Sheffield* website): 1, 2, 3, 5, 6, 15, 18; Sheffield City Archives: 23; Kay Aitch: 4, 7, 8; Adrian and Christine Alker: 54, 86; Roy and Beryl Barry: 85; David Bocking 84; Andrew Braybrook: 22, 31, 33, 34, 35, 37, 62; Pam Broadhurst: 44; Anne and Arthur Button: 82, 83; Cumbrian Newspapers Ltd: 77; Diocese of Sheffield: 50; John Giles: 67; the Revd Sarah Hall: 88; Michael Miller: 76; NADFAS: 24; Northend and Co.: 70; Peter Pace: 45; Tanya Ralph: 94, 95; Richard Taylor: 97, 98, 99; the Revd Shan Rush: picture of history group; Eve Saunders: 75; Sheffield Telegraph and Star: 36, 51, 58, 59, 65, 66; Donald and Josey Smith: 91; the family of the late David Stoker: 81, 89, 93; Charlotte Tonge: 63; and Philip Wright: 100. In addition, we are grateful to Professor Stuart Parker for the picture on the front cover.

Every effort to trace copyright holders of material has been made but St Mark's Church would be grateful to be informed of any omissions.

FOREWORD
by the Bishop of Sheffield

'It was not the place [that was important] but it was the Christian; it was the humble, contrite, prayerful hearts of His people gathered together that constituted a church, and where that church was gathered together there was the presence of Christ among them.'

The words of Thomas Sale, Vicar of Sheffield in 1859 at the first service in St Mark's iron church echo through the story told in these pages. It is a story shaped by many different people over more than 150 years. It is a story shaped by wider events: the immense changes to the city of Sheffield and to Broomhill and Broomhall; the two World Wars (and especially the night of 12 December 1940); the economy of the city, the country and the world. It is a story shaped by the Christian faith, which led to the establishing of a new parish, the shaping of a distinctive Christian community in this place, and the building and rebuilding of a parish church.

At the centre of the story of the modern St Mark's is the story of the response of the congregation, in faith and hope, to the destruction of their building. For 23 years, the St Mark's community persevered in temporary accommodation and looked forward to the building of the new St Mark's. The new building, when it came, looked back to the past, forward to the future and out to the community around. We do our best to shape our church buildings but, in different ways, our church buildings shape us from generation to generation.

Every parish church is home to a rich, textured community of Christian people with its own particular story, who gather together to celebrate God's story from generation to generation. Some have been part of St Mark's for most of their lives. Some are here for a few years before moving on to live and serve elsewhere. St Mark's has played its part in the shaping of this diocese and the wider church and world over the last 50 years.

The history of St Mark's as told here is a valuable resource to the Church in the present day. As we look back, we see the immense challenges with which our predecessors wrestled; we see the way in which great enterprises can grow from modest beginnings; we see conflicts resolved and others begun; we see mission in its many and various forms; we see all that flows from engagement with the scriptures and the celebration of the sacraments; we discern the presence of Christ among God's people in this place.

+Steven Sheffield

INTRODUCTION

David Price

'I wonder how long it takes to grow a congregation like St Mark's?'

The question was posed by the distinguished American biblical scholar, Professor Marcus Borg, at the conclusion of his third visit to St Mark's in 2011. We do not know what led him to ask this question, but assume that he was struck by something distinctive about the worshipping community, its common life and its witness to Jesus Christ.

In part, this book supplies an answer to Borg's question by delving into the history of St Mark's. We hope that this will inform not only the people of St Mark's themselves, but also others interested in ways in which a parish church can change and develop.

But this history also marks the fiftieth anniversary of the opening in 1963 of the much admired church building designed by George Pace (1915-75). The *Pevsner Architectural Guide to Sheffield* says that Pace's design 'brilliantly succeeds in balancing a sympathy with Gothic form with the smooth, hard, mechanical forms of Modernism' and goes on to describe the view from the narthex as 'one of serene beauty'.[1] However, in order to provide context and a sense of continuity, we have deliberately gone back long before this 1960s rebuilding to explore the origins of St Mark's.

The book has been prepared by a team of researchers and writers drawn mainly from the present congregation. We have met frequently in order to ensure a common approach. We have deliberately written in more detail about more recent decades, partly to reflect access to a greater body of source material, but also on the assumption that this period will be of more interest to our readers. Around 100 illustrations have been included.

Among other things, our story highlights how the character of a church is influenced by its external environment. The Victorian St Mark's was built when Sheffield was the greatest cutlery and steel town in the world. The church took on some of the flavour of the prosperous industrial and professional families who then lived in the Broomhill area. No doubt the contemporary St Mark's is influenced by different cultures now defining the parish – the universities, the hospitals and the numerous schools.

The ways in which St Mark's has changed provide the structure of our book. In Chapter 1, Rosie Richards uncovers the previously obscure history of the iron church, which was erected on St Mark's Green in 1859. She describes the early congregation and explains how St Mark's stone church came to be built on an adjacent site, leading to its consecration in 1871. In Chapter 2, Helen Mathers tells the story of the original stone church, its ministers and its congregation through the late Victorian period and the early twentieth century up to the end of the First World War.

In Chapter 3, Tim Moore describes the church during the uncertain inter-war years, before giving an account, in Chapter 4, of the most dramatic event in the history of St Mark's – its destruction by incendiary bombs on the night of 12 December 1940. He then recounts how the congregation, meeting in the Church Hall in Ashgate Road for more than two decades, made strenuous efforts to ensure that St Mark's was rebuilt.

I have contributed the three historical chapters on the period since 1960. Chapter 5 describes the 1960s – an important turning point. Not only was the new church building consecrated in 1963, but in addition, Michael Adie as Vicar set out to build a new congregation with a different ethos from that of the old St Mark's. Chapter 6 tells how Adie's vision was continued and built upon in the ministry of his successors, Michael Paton and John Giles.

Chapter 7 progresses the story of the church into the 1990s and 2000s, during the ministry of Adrian Alker – another remarkable period of change. It was in 2000 that Marcus Borg was invited to speak at the church, leading to the subsequent establishment of the St Mark's Centre for Radical Christianity. In this chapter, people well known to the present congregation are referred to by their Christian names.

In Chapter 8, Michael Hunt, a current Church Warden, draws on a survey of the congregation to describe some of the beliefs and attitudes held by the church community today. In Chapter 9, Richard Taylor writes about 'how to read St Mark's' – in other words how to interpret the symbolism and architecture of the building. In Chapter 10, our present Vicar, the Revd Dr Ian Wallis, offers some 'concluding reflections'.

Our sub-title refers to 'Broomhill and Broomhall'. The geography needs some explanation. The church was known as 'St Mark's Broomhall' from 1859 to 1991, when the legal title 'St Mark's Broomhill' was adopted, which survives to this day. The original reference to 'Broomhall' derived from the parochial district of 'Broomhall', designated in 1846 using the name of the historic mansion of Broom Hall as shorthand for a large suburban area. In 1859, the iron church was established near to the area already known as 'Broomhill'. In the Victorian period, 'Brooomhall' became defined as the area around Broomhall Road, Broomspring Lane and Hanover Street, between Glossop Road and Ecclesall Road. St Mark's parish boundaries narrowed as new churches took over part of the original area. Then in the late twentieth century, they widened again as churches closed. In particular, St Mark's took responsibility for the part of 'Broomhall' west of the Ring Road. In this book, we describe 'church life in Broomhill and Broomhall' in relation to the history of St Mark's Church, with its changing parish boundaries.

Finally, over the years, many people have helped to make St Mark's what it is today. Inevitably, our account has had to be highly selective and cannot do justice to all those valuable individual contributions.

Notes

[1] Ruth Harman and John Minnis, *Pevsner Architectural Guide: Sheffield* (Newhaven, CT: Yale University Press, 2004), p. 249.

CHAPTER 1

ORIGINS – UP TO THE CONSECRATION OF ST MARK'S STONE CHURCH IN 1871

Rosie Richards

Introduction

In the first half of the nineteenth century Sheffield was a rapidly growing industrial town, returning its first elected Members of Parliament only after the 1832 Reform Bill and becoming a city in 1893. In 1801, the total population, including the outlying townships was 45,758, but by 1851 it had risen to 135,310 and continued to rise throughout the century,[1] The population of Broomhill and Broomhall 'grew from 3,120 in 1841 to 7,065 in 1861'.[2]

As far as the Church of England was concerned, Sheffield was still in the Diocese of York as the Diocese of Sheffield was not created until 1914. The building that is now Sheffield Cathedral was the ancient parish church, serving the whole of the town. Although St Paul's, in what is now the Peace Gardens, and St James had been built in the eighteenth century, they were still chapels of ease to the Parish Church and not separate parishes. There was also a large population of Methodists and other Nonconformists, who in the 1850s were more numerous than the Anglicans.

In the nineteenth century, Church of England clergy in Sheffield were predominately Evangelical. E.R. Wickham states that

> the appointment of Thomas Sutton, a strong evangelical churchman, to the living of Sheffield in 1805, which he occupied until his death in 1851, was responsible for a long sequence of evangelical clergy in the parish, and in 1841 the advowson [patronage] was purchased by a few individuals to ensure the appointment of a successor with similar views, with the result that the clergy were much in line with the essential theological outlook of the Nonconformists.[3]

During the nineteenth century, the Church of England experienced various legal, administrative and pastoral reforms, some of which influenced the development of St Mark's. Other influences included the considerable increase in church building and church attendance in Sheffield, particularly among the middle classes, during the second half of the century. The creation of St Mark's was also part of that religious boom.

Concerned about the growing urban population in the country, the Government in 1818 had provided a large sum of money, over £1,000,000, under the 'Million Act' to provide extra churches to house Church of England congregations. In Sheffield, St George's (1825), Christ Church Attercliffe (1826), St Philip's (1828) and St Mary's, Bramall Lane (1830) were built under this scheme.

Furthermore, the Ecclesiastical Commission of the Church of England was made permanent in 1836 and, in addition, a Church Building Act became law in 1843. This 'established a straight forward procedure for sub-dividing [Church of England] parishes'. Prior to this, a separate Act of Parliament had been needed for each subdivision.[4]

As a result, 'The Ecclesiastical Commissioners, with the sanction of the Queen and Privy

Council, determined in 1846 that the large and populous parish of Sheffield should be ecclesiastically divided into 25 parochial districts, each to have a church and an incumbent.[5] Broomhall was one of these districts.

This very extensive area stretched from Hanover Street in the east to Upper Hallam Township in the west; and from Fulwood Road, Broomhill, Northumberland Road and Wilkinson Street in the north and north-east, to the east end of Ecclesall Road and the River Porter in the south and west (See map of parish boundaries on page 16). The District included Broomhall, Endcliffe, the Collegiate School (now part of Sheffield Hallam University), Wesley College (now King Edward VII School), large houses such as the Mount, and the Botanical Gardens.

The boundary of Upper Hallam Township was the Oakbrook, which now runs from north of Fulwood Road into the Porter just below Riverdale Road, so at that time the very large Broomhall District probably also covered what is now part of Endcliffe Park. This part of Sheffield was mainly a wealthy residential area, particularly towards the north and north-west of the District where the affluent middle classes were buying up plots and building houses.

The Beginning of St Mark's

In the early part of the nineteenth century, William Butcher, a wealthy and important steel manufacturer, who lived at Five Oaks, 428 Glossop Road (now demolished for the building of the Royal Hallamshire Hospital), had purchased part of the Broomhill House estate. This included the triangular piece of land, which was then a field and part of Broomfield, and is now enclosed by Beech Hill Road, Broomfield Road, Newbould Lane and Glossop Road. Nowadays, this area comprises St Mark's Green, the Crescent, houses round the Crescent, the present St Mark's Church and the houses on the south side of Broomfield Road.[6]

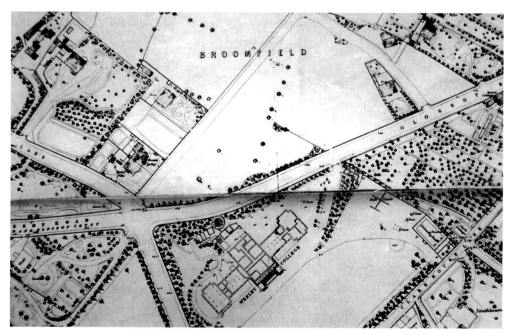

1. Extract from the 1853 Ordnance Survey map of Sheffield showing part of Broomfield, Glossop Road and Wesley College (now King Edward VII School).

2

In 1849 or 1850, William Butcher provided a plot on Broomfield near Glossop Road for the erection of a church to serve the Broomhall District. However, it was about 21 years before St Mark's stone church was finally completed in 1871.

Since the creation of the Broomhall District in 1846, various suggestions had been made to provide a church for the area. Lee and Flockton, a firm of Sheffield architects, drew up several plans, including two for a couple of small stone churches, one for 400 'sittings' costing £900 to £1,000, and another for approximately 450 sittings costing £1,100 to £1,200. Finally, in 1849, the firm produced a design for a much larger church.[7]

Another attempt to move matters forward occurred as a result of a controversy at Sheffield Parish Church. In 1850 one of the Assistant Ministers at the Parish Church died and the Sheffield Church Burgesses appointed Canon George Trevor of York to take his place against the wishes of the Vicar, Dr Thomas Sutton, who refused to accept his appointment – a decision in which Dr Sutton was supported by 26 of the Sheffield clergy. 'It seems that Canon Trevor was an advocate and supporter of the Society for the Propagation of the Gospel in Foreign Parts, a body considered much "too high church" by the evangelically minded Dr. Sutton.'[8]

Dr Sutton died in January 1851 and his successor, Dr Thomas Sale, also vetoed Canon Trevor's appointment. In an attempt to find a way out of this dilemma, it was suggested that Canon Trevor should be appointed to serve in the Broomhall District and that 'a large new Church of 1,000 sittings' should be built – perhaps the one that Lee and Flockton had designed in 1849? but Canon Trevor declined to accept the offer on the terms that were proposed and so the plan was abandoned.[9]

However, as a result of this controversy, the 1554 Charter of the Church Burgesses was amended in 1854 and among the amendments was a provision for the Broomhall District to be endowed at their 'discretion'.[10]

The Building of St Mark's Iron Church in 1859

At the ceremony for the laying of the foundation stone of St Mark's stone church in October 1868, Dr Thomas Sale, who lived at 'Belmonte' (now 34 Collegiate Crescent) in Broomhall, gave a speech in which he set out some of the reasons that had inspired him to erect St Mark's iron church. On becoming Vicar of Sheffield, he realised that the Broomhall District was an 'important and influential section' of the parish, but it was so far from the 'Parish Church that it was utterly impossible pastoral charge could be carried out properly'. There were many people living locally who for a long time had looked forward to having a church in the area, and he was unwilling to 'close his ears to [their] wishes'. He also felt it was important to have a clergyman resident in the district, and he 'was anxious to show that a congregation could be got together at once' and that many people would attend.[11] He was probably also influenced by the fact that a prefabricated building could be in theory demolished and erected elsewhere once a permanent church had been built.

The result was that the temporary corrugated iron church known as St Mark's Church, Broomhall, was erected on Glossop Road on 13 November 1859.[12] 'The land belongs to Mr. W. Butcher and the building was erected by the Vicar [Thomas Sale], Mr. W. Butcher, Mr. S. Butcher, Mr. J.N. Mappin and Mr. H. Rodgers ... Service is performed by the Vicar of the Parish Church and his assistant ministers.'[13] One of these assistant ministers was Samuel Earnshaw, a brilliant and distinguished mathematician, born in Sheffield, who lived at 14 Beech Hill Road.

Thomas Sale had himself raised some of the cost of approximately £1,400-£1,700 and he borrowed the rest from the four local gentlemen mentioned above. It was agreed that these four gentlemen would be repaid out of the pew rents so that ultimately the iron church became Thomas Sale's private property.

The iron church was a chapel of ease to Sheffield Parish Church. However, there is no clear indication in the newspapers or other documents that it was consecrated. The *Sheffield Daily Telegraph* of 14 November 1859 stated:

> The opening service was performed yesterday morning by the Vicar, but no deviation was made from the ordinary form of worship, and not the slightest ceremony was observed in the inauguration of the building. The attendance was exceedingly good and the sermon was listened to with the most marked interest.

It is interesting that Thomas Sale emphasized in his sermon that:

> It was not the place [that was important], but it was the Christian; it was the humble, contrite, prayerful hearts of His people gathered together that constituted a church, and where that church was gathered together there was the presence of Christ amongst them.[14]

An 1864 map of Sheffield covering the area of the 1853 Ordnance Survey map (Fig. 1 above) shows the iron church apparently situated on the eastern side of St Mark's Green on an approximate north/south alignment at right angles to Glossop Road. It can be seen from this map that the Crescent was already in place and that several houses had already been erected round the Crescent, including the present Vicarage, built in 1862.[15] The four other houses shown on the map had been built before the iron church, demonstrating the increasing pressure on building plots as the population increased in this western area of the town.

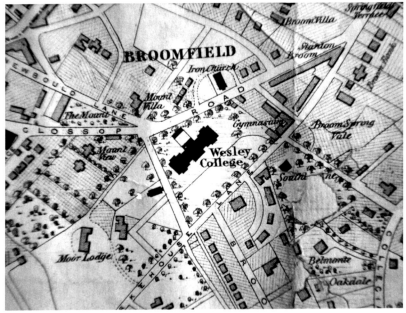

2. **Extract from 1864 map of Sheffield, showing St Mark's iron church.**

4

In 1871, the iron church was moved to Carbrook, and the 1891 Ordnance Survey map of that area shows a ground plan of the iron church, now known as St Bartholomew's, which was situated on the north side of Bright Street. This plan confirms many of the descriptions of the iron church at St Mark's, and also shows the 'east' end of the Carbrook church facing approximately north-west, so maybe people were less concerned with theology and more with practicalities in the siting of this very large building.[16]

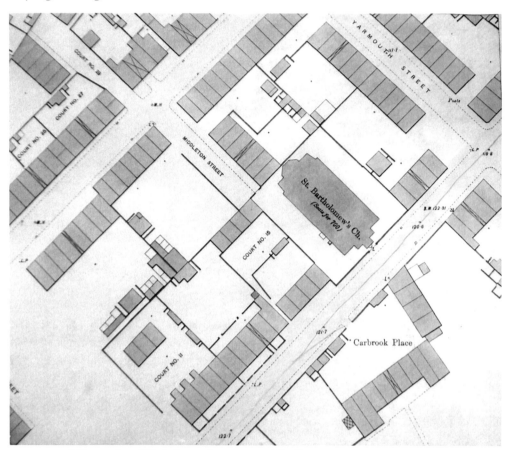

3. Extract from 1891 Ordnance Survey map of Sheffield, showing the iron church in Carbrook, now called St Bartholomew.

The iron church was completed and erected on Glossop Road in about four months by 'Mr. Hemming of Moorgate-street, London', who seems highly likely to have been Samuel Hemming of Bristol and London, an important exporter of prefabricated corrugated iron buildings and churches, especially for the Australian market.[17] It was a very large oblong building – 90 ft long by 50 ft wide 'with side aisles and an apse at the east end for the communion and choir'. It was described as a 'plain Gothic structure, with a small tower and spire, with the usual "churchgoing bell"', and 'with a miniature entrance porch' at the west end which was very close to Glossop Road. Internally, it was described as having a 'light and cheerful appearance', with pews, reading desk, pulpit, organ and communion table. The interior apart from the roof was covered 'with a kind of painted canvas or felt'.[18]

5

'Most of the pews' were described as 'well cushioned and made very comfortable'. Attached to each pew was 'a small umbrella holder', which was helpful as they prevented people's best Sunday dresses from becoming wet after a downpour on the way to church. Some of these descriptions give an insight into the wealth of the congregation:

> These umbrella holders, when occupied by the beautiful silk umbrellas with pearl and ivory handles which abound at the Iron Church, present a very attractive and aristocratic appearance. So do the ledges of the pews, covered with elegant church services, bound in velvet, with gilt rims and handsome monograms. It is really pleasing to observe such signs of taste and opulence.[19]

Criticus – a local journalist, who visited the iron church anonymously in 1869/70 found himself 'amongst the *elite* of the Sheffield church going society. ... There were mayors, aldermen, councillors, solicitors, brewers, merchants and manufacturers, and independent gentlemen.' He was overcome by the ladies:

> so many of them, and so good-looking and so well-dressed, that my powers of description are wholly inadequate … And all were so devout, and so decorous, and so well-behaved that the influence was refining and elevating. There was no looking about, no turning round, no gazing at other's dresses, notwithstanding the attraction and temptation … There were real seal skin and sable, silks and satins, velvets and merinoes. There were every style and description of beauty.

He also mentions that 'There were also not a few attired in "quiet" style with neatness and elegance.'[20]

It is fair to state that, although most of the congregation were very wealthy, they were also very generous:

> That the liberality of the congregation at the Iron Church is equal to their wealth may be seen from the fact that on 'Hospital Sunday' their contributions far exceed those from any other place of worship in the town, and reach over £100.

In 1869, a summary of the Church Accounts indicated that £403.2.5 was given to Medical and Evangelical Church Charities such as the Church Missionary Society. This was a very substantial sum at that time.[21]

The iron church appears to have seated between 570 and 625 people with 35 free seats for the poor. Most of the seats were acquired by people 'able and willing to pay for pews'. However, 'there are not many [poor people] in this locality, and [they]... would be rather out of place in the iron church, although, of course they would be heartily welcomed'.[22]

It seems extraordinary now that people paid for a seat in a church as though they were booking a season ticket for concerts at the City Hall, but it was a well-established method of raising income among many of the denominations, especially where the endowments or stipends were small. The practice was criticized, however, especially by the Anglo-Catholics, and did emphasize the difference between the 'haves' and the 'have nots'.

4. An artist's impression of St Mark's iron church, drawn by Kay Aitch from newspaper descriptions and other sources.

Some Important People

The four men who lent Thomas Sale money to assist him in erecting the iron church were all prominent members of the local community.

The Butcher brothers, William and Samuel, were steel manufacturers who set up a business in Eyre Lane and later at the Philadelphia Works on the River Don, exporting edged tools, knives and files to America. William Butcher was Master Cutler in 1845 and on his death in 1870 left 'effects valued at under £100,000'. Samuel Butcher was a Church Burgess and became Mayor of Sheffield in 1845.[23]

**5. William Butcher (1791?-1870), steel manufacturer and benefactor to St Mark's. He provided the land on which both the iron church and the stone church were built.
Source: Picture Sheffield**

John Newton Mappin was a brewer, who left the whole of his art collection to the town; it was later housed in the Mappin Art Gallery. 'He was a generous contributor to the Church of England', in particular by building the Church of St John the Evangelist in Ranmoor, which was almost totally destroyed by fire in 1887.[24]

Henry Rodgers was a Church Burgess and a solicitor. 'A decided Evangelical ... He was one of the most trusted of Sheffield lawyers, wonderfully courteous and kind, and known to all as a devoted friend of the Church and its clergy.' He was responsible for suggesting that the Revd William Milton, the first incumbent of St Mark's, should come as minister to the Broomhall District. After Henry Rodgers' death in April 1882, William Milton described him in a sermon as 'the wise counsellor, the sympathetic helper, the faithful prayerful friend that I once had ... the loss is irreparable. The place of Mr Henry Rodgers can never again be filled.'[25]

7

Another important person, Arthur Thomas, was a solicitor, a Church Burgess and Henry Rodgers' nephew. 'He was constantly consulted by clergy, churchwardens and other Church officials, and was known as "the parsons' friend" … he was a broad-minded but decided Evangelical, strongly opposed to all Romanizing innovations.' He was the Secretary of the Building Committee of the 1871 stone church, and memorial windows in both the present Cathedral and the 1871 St Mark's were installed in his memory.[26]

Before he came to Sheffield Parish Church in 1851, Dr Thomas Sale, a former Fellow of Magdalen College, Oxford, had been the 'perpetual curate' of Southgate in the parish of Edmonton, London, for 20 years, so he must have had some experience of creating new parochial districts or parishes. Criticus stated that he was 'thoroughly evangelical, free from all eccentricities of doctrine and from ritualistic tendencies … He is broad and liberal in his views and teachings.' He was energetic and tactful, with considerable business ability. His stipend was £500 a year, but it was 'well known' that he gave 'a large part of his income to public and charitable' causes.[27]

6. The Revd Canon Dr Thomas Sale, Vicar of Sheffield from 1851 to 1873. He played a crucial role in getting both the iron church and the stone church built.
Source: Picture Sheffield

The Appointment of the Revd William Milton

In his speech at the laying of the foundation stone of St Mark's stone church in October 1868, Dr Thomas Sale congratulated the congregation on the progress made in erecting a permanent church for the Broomhall District. However, he also expressed his frustration that this had taken so long. He had estimated that six years would be sufficient time to reimburse all the benefactors, and that the iron church could then have been removed elsewhere. 'The end of six years came, and the money was paid off, but he was sorry to say there was very little preparation made to build a church at all.' He had apparently dropped hints that he would remove the iron church if nothing happened, although he said he would not in fact have done so. He had then realized that the congregation would never get a permanent church until they found a clergyman whom they trusted would not 'carry out those ritualistic proceedings which had disgusted so many of the laity'.[28]

In 1867, Thomas Sale's friend, the Revd William Milton, preached at St Mark's iron church as part of a deputation from the Church Pastoral Aid Society. The congregation liked him and asked if he could become their minister. However, they were told by Thomas Sale that they must first endow the District and second be prepared to build a church.

Around 14 March 1867, William Milton left his former largely 'artisan' parish of Christ Church, New Radford, Nottingham, where he had been the 'perpetual curate' for 22 years, and came to St Mark's iron church.[29] The endowment of £150 'was a great difficulty', but after negotiation was provided partly by the Church Burgesses and partly by subscription from the congregation, and augmented by pew rents to £300 per annum. It also appears that, in 1867, the Broomhall District was 'legally constituted' as the District of St Mark Broomhall but did not officially become a parish until the permanent stone church was consecrated in 1871. The part of the endowment raised by subscription from the congregation appears to have included rents from land and properties in

Upperthorpe, which were conveyed to the Ecclesiastical Commissioners on 15 July 1867.[30]

When Criticus visited the iron church in 1869/70, he wrote that the lessons were read 'with distinctness, correctness, and good taste' by a young man. He described this practice as 'unusual' and as 'the introduction of the lay element into the services of the church'. On this particular Sunday morning, the *Te Deum* was sung by choir and congregation, the Litany began at 11.10, and then a hymn was sung 'before the Communion Service, which was read by the Rev. W. Milton, and responded to by the choir and congregation. The prayers were over at 11.40, when another hymn was sung, and the sermon began at 11.45' and did not finish until 12.20, making a service of at least one-and-a-half hours. The choir was described as 'very unpretending' and the congregation joined in the singing 'more heartily and more devoutly than is usual in most churches'. About 400 people attended the service, 'a goodly proportion of whom were ladies'.

William Milton was described as being 'somewhat advanced in years', but possessing 'great energy and an exuberance of vivacity on suitable occasions … he is admirably adapted to his congregation with whom he is deservedly very popular … He is thoroughly evangelical and abhors ritualism.' The congregation 'agree with Mr Milton on the importance and propriety of religious conservatism. They are not generally inclined to be radicals either in religion or politics.'[31]

Laying the Foundation Stone of St Mark's Stone Church, 28 October 1868

There is no doubt that William Milton's appointment stimulated the congregation into making plans to erect a permanent stone church. An 'influential' Building Committee was formed; in 1868 an appeal was launched to raise funds to erect the building and a list of subscriptions was published, showing that £7,600 had already been promised.[32]

However, a problem presented itself. Originally '...It was intended that the new church should be built on the site of the iron church; but Mr. Butcher, to suit the convenience of the congregation, received back his first gift of land and gave a second and larger' site, where the present St Mark's now stands.[33]

As all the sittings in the iron church had been let since the church was opened, and with the growing population in the district, it was obviously thought that a bigger church was needed. It was probably also thought desirable to use the iron church for services while the stone church was being constructed. What is now St Mark's Green must have remained in private ownership for about 60 years until 1933, when it was sold for £450 by William Butcher Hall, presumably a descendant of William Butcher's younger daughter, to the Sheffield Diocesan Trust and Board of Finance for the use of St Mark's parish.[34]

On 28 October 1868, a beautiful day, the foundation stone of St Mark's stone church was laid by Mrs Rosa Cutler, the wife of John Edward Cutler and oldest surviving daughter of William Butcher, who was unable to attend through 'indisposition'. A large number of people were present, including the Revd William Milton, the Revd Dr Thomas Sale, Mr John Webster, Mayor of Sheffield, Rosa's husband and Henry Rodgers, who were Churchwardens, William Henry Crossland, the architect, and John Chambers and Son, the builders of the church.

After prayers and singing a hymn, Arthur Thomas, the Secretary of the Building Committee, presented Mrs Cutler with a trowel and a mallet made by Messrs Walker and Hall of Sheffield. She was also given 'a bottle to be deposited in a cavity of the stone' containing two local newspapers, coins of the realm and a parchment containing the history of the church, 'its dedication, assignment and patronage'. The parchment apparently stated that the church was dedicated to St John the Evangelist on land given by William Butcher, the District of St Mark, Broomhall, Sheffield, was created in 1867, the Church Burgesses were the patrons, and the church was to be built by public subscription. After Mrs Cutler had performed the ceremony, and Dr Sale had given his speech, the Committee and other dignitaries had lunch with Mr Butcher at his house on Glossop Road.[35]

The Consecration of St Mark's Church, Wednesday 31 May 1871

On 31 May 1871, the church was opened at 11a.m. and the congregation was so large that almost every seat was taken. The Archbishop of York, accompanied by a large number of clergy, met in the iron church and processed up the centre aisle, the Archbishop 'passing inside the Communion rails' while most of the clergy sat in the transepts. The Mayor, Mr Thomas Moore, and Sir John Brown, the prominent industrialist, were also in the procession. Criticus noted that the Mayor 'wore his chain of office and a scarlet robe trimmed with sable' – the first time a Mayor of Sheffield had appeared in his robes on any official occasion. After the service, the Archbishop, clergy, the Mayor and Sir John Brown all had lunch at Five Oaks on Glossop Road, by then the home of Rosa and John Edward Cutler, as William Butcher had died in November 1870.[36]

Services were also held in the church over the following days, and total collections amounting to £330 were taken in an attempt to clear the debt on the church and to purchase a new organ in place of the temporary organ from the iron church.

The *Sheffield Daily Telegraph* of 29 October 1868 and 1 June 1871 stated that the church was to be dedicated to St John the Evangelist. We do not know what lay behind the decision to retain St Mark as the church's patron saint.

William Henry Crossland (1835-1908), the architect of the church, was a pupil of Sir George Gilbert Scott and specialized in Gothic designs. He was first in practice in Huddersfield and Halifax but later worked in Leeds and in London. In addition to St Mark's, he designed a number of other churches and commercial buildings, notably Rochdale Town Hall. After moving to London, his important commissions were a middle-class asylum in Surrey for the philanthropist Thomas Holloway, and also Royal Holloway College at Egham (now part of London University).[37]

The new St Mark's was a very large grand building, with seats for about 900 people. Criticus described the inside of the church as having a 'light, elegant and cheerful appearance', as, apart from the east end chancel window dedicated to Dr Samuel Parker of Broomgrove before Criticus' visit in 1873, none of the stained glass was installed until the 1880s or 1890s. The corona of 70 lights in the chancel was 'magnificent … and the effect, at night is strikingly beautiful. In the evening the church is lighted by twelve 36-light coronae.'[38]

The church received some very expensive gifts. For example, the reredos extended the whole width of the chancel, the centre piece in Caen stone representing the Last Supper, with 'emblems' of the Evangelists on either side 'let into slabs of Devonshire spar'. Above the reredos were carved figures of angels and underneath was the inscription 'To the glory of God, and in memory of Wm. Butcher, of Five Oaks, who died November 8, 1870; erected in loving remembrance by his daughter, Rosa Elizabeth, and her husband, John Edward Cutler.'[39]

The pulpit, the gift of Mrs Sarah Waterhouse of Broomgrove, was composed of 'richly carved alabaster arches supported by pillars of green Connemara marble [on] a pedestal of Caen stone', with a carved oak sounding board. Miss Mountain of Collegiate Crescent gave an 'altar cloth of crimson silk velvet' for the 'Communion table' and Mrs John Wing of Glossop Road gave 'a complete set of books … richly bound in morocco'.

7. The Last Supper – the central section of the reredos, drawn by Kay Aitch from photographs.

8. The pulpit in the 1871 St Mark's Church, drawn by Kay Aitch from photographs.

The pews, with their umbrella holders at the ends, were 'comfortable and commodious, sloping backs, cushioned, carpeted and provided with hassocks'. The free seats were 'furnished in the same way as the others [i.e. the rented seats], the authorities at St Mark's wisely refusing to distinguish the poor by putting them on hard benches or in an inferior place'.[41]

The contract price for building the church was £7,000 but the final price appears to have been £11,000-£12,000. The difference was the cost of providing 'expensive fittings' including 'a wall, surmounted by elegant iron railings, which enclose the ornamental grounds surrounding the Church; the gas apparatus, the warming apparatus (heated by hot water on the high pressure principle) … and the approaches to the Church'. The church was approached 'by a broad flight of stone steps right and left from the south side', although there was also an entrance from Broomfield Road.[42]

As far as can be ascertained from Parish records and other sources, the boundaries of the new parish were exactly the same as those of the 1846 Broomhall District referred to earlier (see map of parish boundaries on page 16). A slight boundary adjustment with the neighbouring parish of

11

St Silas probably took place around 1871 and, as more parishes were created, further boundary changes occurred.[43]

The new St Mark's was in use from the very beginning. The first wedding took place in June 1871, and the early parish registers show that parishioners from a wide diversity of occupations, ranging from manufacturers to artisans and gardeners, were using the church for weddings and baptisms.[44]

The Later History of the Iron Church

The iron church was pulled down in June 1871 and conveyed by drays to Carbrook, where it was renamed St Bartholomew's and re-erected in Bright Street on a site purchased by Dr Thomas Sale. The total cost was about £1,000, but all the seats were free. The church, which looked exactly the same as it did on Glossop Road, was opened on 17 January 1872 and served as a chapel of ease to Christ Church, Attercliffe. Unfortunately, it deteriorated rapidly on account of the 'foreign elements issuing from the large iron and steel furnaces in the neighbourhood'.[45] Taking the building down and re-erecting it must have added to the deterioration, and by 1889 the building was becoming 'exceedingly comfortless'.[46] A permanent St Bartholomew's Church was consecrated in 1891. The iron church must have been taken down sometime afterwards, as the 1903 Ordnance Survey map shows a blank space in the place where it had been erected.[47]

Notes

[1] E.R. Wickham, *Church and People in an Industrial City* (London, 1957), p. 20.
[2] Information from Mrs Eva Wilkinson of Broomhill.
[3] Wickham, *Church and People in an Industrial City*, p. 82.
[4] Gerald Parsons, *Religion in Victorian Britain*, Vol. 1: *Traditions* (Manchester, 1988), p. 22.
[5] William White, *General Directory of the Town and Borough of Sheffield* (Sheffield, 1860), p. 2a.
[6] Information from Mrs Eva Wilkinson. 1853 Ordnance Survey map of Sheffield, Sheets 24 and 29
[7] South Yorkshire County Archive Service, 1-100 SY19 – proposed designs of St Mark's Broomhall by Lee and Flockton 1846-1849, Sheffield City Archives, Ref: SY20/B1/2/3/4.
[8] George Tolley, *We, of our Bounty. A History of the Sheffield Church Burgesses* (Sheffield, 1999), p. 83.
[9] Tolley, *We, of our Bounty*, p. 83.
[10] Tolley, *We, of our Bounty*, p. 41.
[11] *Sheffield Daily Telegraph*, 29 October 1868.
[12] *Sheffield Independent*, 19 November 1859; *Sheffield Daily Telegraph*, 14 November 1859; Criticus 'The Churches and Chapels of Sheffield, their Ministers and Congregations' (cuttings from *The Sheffield Times*, 1869, 1870 and 1871), Sheffield City Archives, Ref: JC 1303, p. 50.
[13] Pawson & Brailsford, *Illustrated Guide to Sheffield and Neighbourhood* [1862], new edition edited by Mary Walton (Wakefield, 1971) p. 45.
[14] *Sheffield Daily Telegraph*. 14 November 1859.
[15] Map of the Town and Environs of Sheffield in the West Riding of the County of York 1864, Lithographed by Pawson & Brailsford, S2R and S6R (Sheffield Local Studies Library). Information from Mrs Eva Wilkinson.
[16] 1891 Ordnance Survey map of Sheffield CCXCV.I.3. Information from Ms Ann Sapcote of Attercliffe.
[17] Adam Mornement and Simon Holloway, *Corrugated Iron: Building on the Frontier* (London, 2007) pp. 81-83, 90, 100; M.M. Chrimes (ed.), *Biographical Dictionary of Civil Engineers in Great Britain and Ireland*, Vol. 2: *1830-1890* (London, 2008), pp. 396-7; *Sheffield Daily Telegraph*, 14 November 1859; Criticus (Newspaper cuttings including 'The Preachers of Sheffield' by Criticus, 'Local Sketches' by Scrutator etc.) Sheffield City Archives Ref: JC 1305, p. 39 (*The Sheffield Post*, 26 July 1873).
[18] *Sheffield Daily Telegraph*, 14 November 1859; Criticus JC 1303, p. 50.
[19] Criticus, JC 1303, p. 50.
[20] Criticus, JC 1303, p. 50.

[21] Criticus, JC 1303, p. 52; *St Mark's Church 1871-1921* (Sheffield, 1921), pp. 12, 13.

[22] *Sheffield Independent*, 19 November 1859, Criticus, JC 1303, pp. 50, 51 and JC 1305, p. 39.

[23] Tolley, *We, of our Bounty*, p. 200; Geoffrey Tweedale, *Giants of Sheffield Steel The Men Who Made Sheffield the Steel Capital of the World* (n.p., 1986), pp. 20-8.

[24] William Odom, *Hallamshire Worthies: Characteristics and Work of Notable Sheffield Men and Women* (Sheffield, 1926), pp. 96, 97.

[25] Odom, *Hallamshire Worthies*, pp. 140, 141; Tolley, *We, of our Bounty*, p. 232; *Sheffield Daily Telegraph*, 27 September 1884; William Milton, 'Address to the congregation of St Mark's Broomhall, Sheffield, together with a statement of account, 1881 to 1882' (1882). Sheffield Local Studies Library, Local pamphlets, Vol: 10. No.18, pp. 9, 10.

[26] Odom, *Hallamshire Worthies*, pp. 142, 143; Tolley, *We, of our Bounty*, p. 241; *Sheffield Daily Telegraph*, 29 October 1868; William Odom, *Memorials of Sheffield: Its Cathedral and Parish Churches* (Sheffield, 1922), p. 180.

[27] Odom, *Hallamshire Worthies*, pp. 52, 53; Criticus, JC 1303, p. 17.

[28] *Sheffield Daily Telegraph*, 29 October 1868.

[29] *Sheffield Daily Telegraph*, 27 September 1884, and 20 March 1867.

[30] Joseph Hunter, *Hallamshire*, new edition with additions by Rev. Alfred Gatty D.D. (Sheffield, 1869), p. 283; *Sheffield Daily Telegraph*, 29 October 1868; Criticus, JC 1305, p. 39; William White, *Directory of the Boroughs of Sheffield* (Sheffield, 1868), pp. 12, 76. The original documents of the Conveyance 29 February 1868, Petition 1871, and Sentence of Consecration 31 May 1871, are held at Sheffield Diocesan Registry; *Formation of Ecclesiastical Districts* – Information Sheet from the Ecclesiastical Commissioners 1899/1900. Box 130 DRB/2/2 uncatalogued material (Sheffield City Archives); St Mark's Parish Registers PR 133: Register of Baptisms PR(m) 133/1, pp. 1, 6; Register of Marriages PR(m) 133/3, p. 1 (Sheffield City Archives); Criticus JC 1303, p. 52.

[31] Criticus, JC 1303, pp. 50, 51.

[32] *Sheffield Daily Telegraph*, 27 September 1884 and 29 October 1868; *St Mark's Church 1871-1921*, pp. 3, 5.

[33] Criticus, JC 1305, p. 39; Conveyance 29 February 1868 (see n. 30 above).

[34] Criticus, JC 1305, p. 39. Information from Mrs Eva Wilkinson, and copy Conveyance dated 10 April 1933 held at St Mark's Vicarage.

[35] *Sheffield Daily Telegraph*, 29 October 1868; *Sheffield Independent*, 29 October 1868; Criticus, JC 1305, p. 37 (*The Sheffield Post*, 19 July 1873).

[36] Criticus, JC 1305, p. 37; *Sheffield Independent*, 1 June 1871; *Sheffield Daily Telegraph*, 1 June 1871.

[37] Derek Linstrum, *West Yorkshire Architects and Architecture* (London, 1978), p. 375, and see the entry under Crossland, William Henry in the *Oxford Dictionary of National Biography*.

[38] Criticus, JC 1305, pp. 37, 38 (*The Sheffield Post*, 19 July 1873); *Sheffield Independent*, 1 June 1871; Odom, *Memorials of Sheffield*, pp. 180, 181.

[39] Odom, *Memorials of Sheffield*, p. 179; Criticus, JC 1305, p. 38, *Sheffield Daily Telegraph*, 1 June 1871. Information from Mrs Eva Wilkinson.

[40] Odom, *Memorials of Sheffield*, p. 179; Criticus, JC 1305, p. 38; *Sheffield Independent*, 1 June 1871; William White, *General and Commercial Directory of Sheffield* (Sheffield, 1871), p. 51.

[41] Criticus, JC 1305, p. 38.

[42] Criticus, JC 1305, p. 39; *Sheffield Independent*, 1 June 1871; 1890 Ordnance Survey map of Sheffield CCXCIV.II.3 and CCXCIV.II.2; William White, *General and Commercial Directory of Sheffield and Rotherham* (Sheffield, 1876), p.76; White, *Directory of Sheffield* (1871), p. 18; *Sheffield Daily Telegraph*, 1 June 1871.

[43] St Mark's Parish Registers – Register of Baptisms PR(m) 133/1, Register of Marriages PR(m) 133/3 (see n. 30 above). White, *Directory of Sheffield* (1871), p. 16; White, *Directory of Sheffield* (1876), p. 74.

[44] St Mark's Parish Registers (see n. 30 above).

[45] *Bradbury's Almanack and General Advertiser* (Sheffield, 1893), p. ii.

[46] *Bradbury's Almanack* (1893), p. iv.

[47] *Sheffield Independent*, 18 January 1872; *Sheffield Daily Telegraph*, 18 January 1872. See *Bradbury's Almanack* (1893), pp. i-iv, for a descriptive article about St Bartholomew's, Carbrook, from the transfer of the iron church in 1872 to the consecration of the new church in 1891. See also Ordnance Survey maps of Sheffield 1891, CCXCV.I.3 and 1903, CCXCV.I.3.z

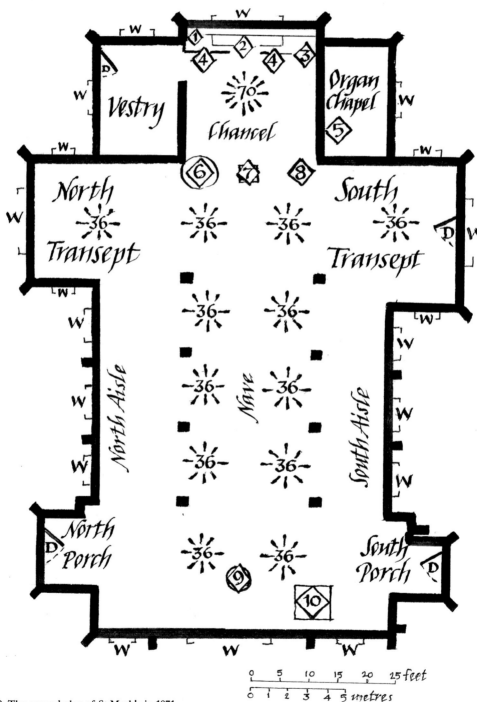

St. Mark's Church 1871 *estimated from various sources*

Vestry

Chancel

Organ Chapel

North Transept

South Transept

North Aisle

Nave

South Aisle

North Porch

South Porch

9. The ground plan of St Mark's in 1871.

St. Mark's Church 1871

Spire   – rising from a tower to 160 feet

Nave   – 96 feet long and 24 feet wide

Aisles   –14 feet 6 inches wide

Transepts – project 17 feet beyond aisle walls
              and 24 feet wide

Chancel - 30 feet by 24 feet

Seating for about 900

1   Reredos   – 'The Last Supper' in Caen stone
                  and Devonshire spar

2   Communion Table

3   Sedilla   – in Caen stone

4   Altar Rails – in brass

5   Organ   – 1871 organ from the Iron Church
                 1879 new organ

6   Pulpit   – in Alabaster and Connemara
                      marble

7   Eagle Lectern – in brass

8   Reading Desk

9   Font   – in Caen stone and marble

10   Tower, supporting the Spire

     70 – corona of 70 lights

     36 – corona of 36 lights

     W – window   D – door

10. The key to the plan on the facing page.

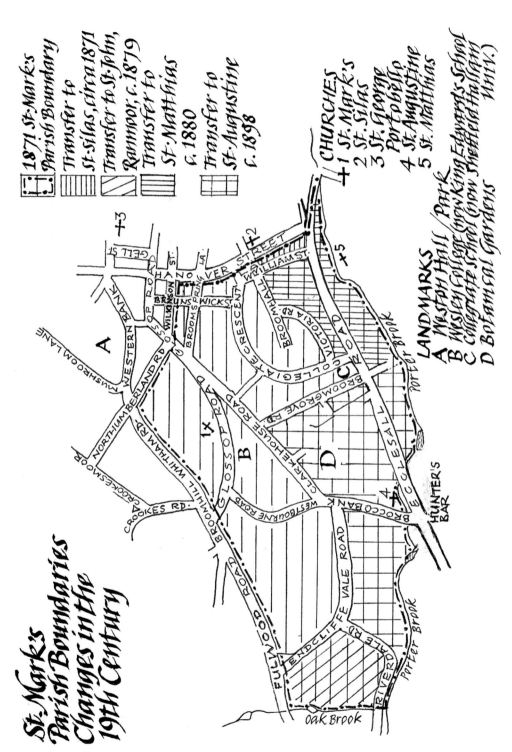

St. Mark's Parish Boundaries Changes in the 19th Century

Key:
- 1871 St. Mark's Parish Boundary
- Transfer to St. Silas, circa 1871
- Transfer to St. John, Ranmoor, c. 1879
- Transfer to St. Matthias c. 1880
- Transfer to St. Augustine c. 1898

CHURCHES
- 1 St. Mark's
- 2 St. Silas
- 3 St. George
- Portobello
- 4 St. Augustine
- 5 St. Matthias

LANDMARKS
- A Weston Hall / Park
- B Wesley College (now King Edward's School
- C Collegiate School (now Sheffield High School VHIV.)
- D Botanical Gardens

11. Map of the 19th century parish boundaries.

16

CHAPTER 2

THE EARLY YEARS OF THE STONE CHURCH, 1871-1919

Helen Mathers

The Ministry of William Milton

The prospect of the new St Mark's was an inviting one. The congregation had an immensely impressive new building that was large enough for their needs. The 1873 drawing (see Frontispiece) shows the 160-foot spire, the two wide doorways and the inviting steps to the terrace. The congregation were greeted at the south porch, making a parade across the terrace from the steps an enjoyable necessity. A gentleman in morning dress escorts two ladies in full crinolines on their approach to the steps; a classic Victorian horse-drawn carriage overtakes them. One had to be wealthy to own a carriage and St Mark's was a fashionable place for the wealthy to worship. Indeed, it quickly acquired the reputation, according to Criticus, of being a 'religious Vanity Fair'[1] – not a flattering description since it suggests excessive attachment to worldly things.

The congregation, always generous in every good (especially evangelical) cause, would have been hurt by this assumption. Moreover, St Mark's had a minister whose roots lay far outside fashionable society and whose Christian standards were high. William Milton graduated from Worcester College, Oxford, with a BA in 1839 and MA in 1842. His first curacy was in the demanding parish of Dewsbury in West Yorkshire, where overwork caused his health to give way. Later he accepted the 'perpetual curacy' at Christ Church in New Radford, Nottingham, a 'forlorn outlying district' where the working-class parishioners supported the radical politics of Chartism and 'clergymen were so unpopular that they were hooted as they passed along the streets'.[2] There was no proper church building, but in his 21 years there Milton secured local sponsors and raised funds to build not only a church but schools as well. This was a time when the church made a vital contribution to the education of working-class children – for many, it was the only schooling they received. By the time Milton left Nottingham, his achievements were so appreciated that 600 people attended a farewell tea, where the Mayor led the eulogies. Milton was presented with several generous gifts including 'the furniture and fittings for a dining-room library'.[3]

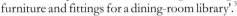

Milton's experience of church building was of great value to the St Mark's congregation, and he had a wonderful ally in Henry Rodgers, who had proposed his appointment to the church and became a close friend.[4] In the new stone church, Milton's ministry was a success. When Criticus returned in 1873, he reported: 'I have rarely met a clergyman who possesses so completely the confidence and the love of his flock'. Milton's preaching style was 'solid and substantial':

He has an excellent voice, and speaks with warmth and earnestness. He is animated and energetic, turns to the right and left, duly dividing his discourse between nave, aisle and transepts ... His sermons are not over-burdened with theological disquisitions, or splitting of doctrinal straws. ... His congregation is composed of

12. The Revd William Milton, first Vicar of St Mark's 1867-84.

gentlemen who have to think hard all the week, and of ladies who are not given to excogitating abstruse problems. They do not expect when they come to church to be set to cracking hard theological nuts for the sake of the kernels of truth.[5]

His preaching was not of the hell-fire variety: Criticus commented drily that 'he does not excite his congregation to external enthusiasm – for well bred people never express or exhibit their emotions'. This was Anglican Evangelicalism expressed in a very decorous form but with 'a vast undercurrent of sympathy, admiration and devotion'.[6] Its theology was conservative and at this date was defined by what it was not – that is, not ritualist. Milton had 'nothing ritualistic about him, either in dress, speech, genuflexion or ideas'.[7] This probably means that he wore a gown, without a surplice, to preach. The gown had become a litmus test of Evangelical commitment, challenged by a Privy Council ruling in 1871 that the surplice must be worn throughout the service. Milton also insisted on the tradition that the psalms were read, rather than intoned or sung.

One of Milton's most fervent preaching themes was support for the mission field, especially the work of the Zenana Mission and the Church Missionary Society (for which he was the local secretary). This was a call to which the congregation always responded. Fund-raising for the new parish was also successful. After his experience in New Radford, Milton was keen to build schools and a parish room. In 1872, he launched an appeal for

> a building for Sunday Schools, Bible classes, cottage lectures, evening gatherings of adults for religious instruction, meetings for district visitors, sewing parties ....[and a] large room in which a public meeting can be held, or a lecture given on useful, scientific or religious matters.[8]

The Parish Rooms on Ashgate Road opened in 1875, with a special service and a festival, for which the tickets cost one shilling on the first day and were 'by invitation only' on the second. Both events sound rather exclusive. The Mutual Improvement Society, which had a large membership during Milton's time, and after it, provided a wide range of activities for the congregation, including public lectures, musical evenings and Bible classes.[9] 'Tableaux vivants', motionless scenes with elaborately costumed characters, were staged in certain years, no doubt after extensive preparation. These were so popular that performances had to be repeated.[10] The Mutual Improvement Society held around 25 meetings a year, mostly in the autumn and winter with a summer seaside excursion and an annual tea and concert. Milton hoped that the public lectures would attract working men, and was disappointed that more did not 'avail themselves of its advantages'. He also offered a Young Women's Bible Class, requesting that 'every mistress would encourage their domestics to avail themselves of this precious opportunity'.[11]

The congregation also financed a splendid new vicarage on land on Melbourne Avenue given by the churchwarden David Ward. This was a substantial gift to the church, and both the grounds and house survive to show his generosity and the pretensions of the church. It was, however, too grand for Milton, who never moved into it. He was ill by the time it was ready, in 1882, and in an address to

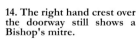

13. **The original St Mark's Vicarage, 5 Melbourne Avenue. It was extended in the early 1900s when Bishop Quirk was the incumbent. It was sold in 1924 and later further enlarged for use as a college. It now belongs to Sheffield High School for Girls.**

14. **The right hand crest over the doorway still shows a Bishop's mitre.**

the congregation that year he said that he preferred money to be spent on good causes. He dwelt on recent bereavements, especially those of friends such as Henry Rodgers and Theophilus Marsh, which had overwhelmed him.[12] Milton's illness forced him to retire in November 1883 at the age of 71, and he died the following year. His funeral at St Mark's concluded with the 'Dead March' from *Saul* and a procession lead by the Archdeacon and local clergy, followed by the choir, 'the boys wearing college caps'.[13]

The Choir and Organ

This choir had improved since 1870 when Criticus had described it as 'very unpretending'. On his return visit in 1873, he found that the music was 'considerably superior', although he noted drily that at some churches 'the music eclipses the preaching; but there is no danger whatever of the one overshadowing the other at St Marks'.[14] The choir numbered about 30, and was composed of 'chubby-faced boys', young men, and older men who in some cases rivalled Milton 'in whitened hair and whiskers'. They wore surplices, which was a fashionable innovation for Evangelical churches. The organist and choirmaster was A. Healey Foster, who must have been delighted by the installation of a new organ in 1879. He served the church for 30 years, until 1900, and was followed by W. Blake Burdekin. The service of their successor, John Arthur Rodgers (1911-20), was commemorated in a bronze and alabaster tablet in the chancel.

The 1881 Religious Census

On 20 November 1881, an attendance census of all the Sheffield churches was taken. St Mark's had 900 sittings available, with 70% full in the morning and 68% in the evening.[15] This was quite impressive, although several churches, especially Christ Church, Pitsmoor, and St Peter's, Heeley, did better. The largest number of sittings were at the so-called 'Million' churches, built to increase the accommodation in working-class areas. St George's, Portobello, for example, had 1,800 sittings, with an attendance in the morning of 58% and evening of 78%. At that date, St George's was surrounded by tiny terraced streets and its parish included some of Sheffield's worst slum housing. Its vicar was clearly a man of exceptional talent. He became the next vicar of St Mark's.

Henry Arnold Favell 1884-96

Henry Favell was the son of a local doctor, Charles Fox Favell, and was born in Norfolk Street in 1845. He was educated at Sheffield Collegiate School and Caius College, Cambridge, and held a curacy in Birmingham before returning to Sheffield in 1873 as Vicar of St George's. He transformed

the church in the ten years he spent there. By 1883, he was in need of a less demanding parish: on his appointment to St Mark's he told his congregation that 'he doubted whether he could continue longer the strain of the last few years' and that he needed 'more time for quiet reading, thought and prayer'.[16]

Favell was 'a big man with a big heart': an 'extremely lovable' character, who greeted everyone he met with an 'unfailing nod', although he often found it hard to remember their names.[17] He also had 'great business ability' and was clearly an outstanding catch for St Mark's. His theology was identical to Milton's, since he 'represented Evangelical theology at its very best' but was tolerant of diverse

15. The Revd Henry Arnold Favell, Vicar 1884-96.
(Source: Picture Sheffield, www.picturesheffield.com).

views.[18] His support for the Church Pastoral Aid Society and the Church Missionary Society was just as zealous as Milton's, and during his time at St Mark's the congregation's giving continued to be unsurpassed. The church often topped the Sheffield donations list on Hospital Sunday, for example.

Favell was also a highly eloquent preacher with a 'magnificent voice'.[19] The respectable folk of St Mark's must have thrilled to his ministrations and been delighted when he was promoted to an honorary canonry at York Minster in 1890. He received several tempting offers to move, including 'more than one colonial bishopric', but he preferred to stay in his native city.[20] In 1895, he was chosen to succeed the highly popular J.E. Blakeney as Archdeacon of Sheffield – a role that he combined with the incumbency of St Mark's.

Stained Glass and Supporters

By 1895, the interior of the church, described as 'light' on its opening in 1871, was more opulent, and considerably darker. A plethora of stained glass windows had been installed as memorials to loved members of the St Mark's congregation. The ground floor plan (see page 14) shows the location of these windows. The vast majority were erected between 1882 and 1897. (See Appendix 3 for descriptions.)

The Marsh family began this trend, since it was Jane Marsh who gave the first window in memory of her father, Samuel Parker, who died in 1871. Jane's husband, Theophilus Marsh, was churchwarden from 1873 to 1878. When Theophilus died in 1881, followed by Jane in 1884, their children erected two panels in the north transept. At the same time, a large window in the south transept 'composed of scenes from the life of our Lord' was dedicated to the memory of William Milton.[21] In the south transept, the life of Arthur Thomas, Parish Warden and Secretary of the Building Committee, was commemorated. A solicitor, he was only 45 when he died in 1884 and was deeply mourned as one of the 'ablest leaders' of the local church.[22] He was a Church Burgess, trustee and treasurer to several societies, and a preacher at mission services.

The 'great central window' at the west end, showing the adoration of Christ by the shepherds and wise men, was presented by John Edward Cutler in 1892.[23] Cutler's wife, Rosa, was the daughter of William Butcher, who donated the land on which St Mark's was built. The Cutlers had already presented the ornate reredos (see pages 10-11) to the new St Mark's, and the west window was another outstandingly generous gift from Cutler alone, since his wife died in 1885. He subsequently gave a clock and a carved oak screen to the church. A director of William Jessop and Sons, J.E. Cutler was one of the late-Victorian generation of philanthropic steel manufacturers who contributed so much to the social fabric of their city. He was a magistrate, and chairman of the Sheffield Savings Bank, the Jessop Hospital for Women and the Charity School for Poor Girls, as well as a colonel in the Hallamshire Rifles, a volunteer regiment.

David Ward, the proprietor of Ward and Payne, was another example of a local steel manufacturer who was devoted to St Mark's and to his city. He was a church warden for many years, Master Cutler in 1877 and Lord Mayor in 1878. He died suddenly in 1889 and his wife presented 'a very handsome silver Communion-service' to the church in his memory.[24]

The Deaths of the Favells and the Building of St Augustine's

The lower west window depicted a Resurrection scene and was dedicated to Mary Favell, who died on 9 December 1894. This tremendous blow to her husband was followed by his own illness, probably cancer.[25] He carried on working until a painful relapse caused his death at the age of only 51 on 26 September 1896. His popularity, and the fact that he had recently been promoted to Archdeacon, made Favell's death a tragedy for the entire Sheffield church community. He was laid to rest in Fulwood churchyard after a crowded funeral at St Mark's conducted by the Bishops of

Beverley and Hull, and Favell's curates T.C. Davies and N.S. Fox.

In the north transept two windows depicting prophets, martyrs, apostles and saints were erected to his memory. Favell's 'most enduring tribute', however, lies elsewhere – and fortunately that one survived World War II.[26]

Favell's dream was of a new church for the growing suburbs of Endcliffe; he secured a site on Brocco Bank and raised £8,000 towards the building costs before his death.[27] His heart was so completely in this project that, on his deathbed, he wrote, 'If I could only see the church in Brocco Bank finished, I could say *Nunc Dimittis* ['Lord, now lettest Thou Thy servant depart in peace'].[28] Shortly after his death, a meeting in the Parish Rooms decided unanimously that 'no more suitable memorial' could be devised than the completion of this church.[29] A meeting at the Cutlers' Hall 'attended by most of the Sheffield clergy and by many prominent Sheffield men' came to the same conclusion.[30] The cost of building the 'Favell Memorial Church' was quickly raised, with a subscription list headed by Sir Henry Stephenson and Sir Frederick Mappin.

The corner stone was laid on 4 July 1897 and the church was named St Augustine's to commemorate Augustine's appointment in 597 as the first Archbishop of Canterbury. It was consecrated 17 months later, on 11 December 1898. St Augustine's is one of the best examples of the work of the church architect, John Dodsley Webster, who was himself a people's warden at St Mark's. A large brass plaque near the chancel arch commemorated Archdeacon Favell as 'the pious founder of this church'. Several members of the St Mark's congregation contributed generously to the furnishings, notably J.E. Cutler, who presented the carved oak communion table, with a reredos depicting the Last Supper. The pulpit was the gift of Favell's sister, Eliza, and the brass eagle lectern was donated by Mrs Arthur Thomas.

16. St Augustine's Church, Brocco Bank, Endcliffe, known as the 'Favell Memorial Church'.

Alfred Pearson 1897-1905

When St Augustine's opened, the parish was divided (see map of parish boundaries on page 16). The area below Clarkehouse Road, from Broomgrove Road onwards, became the responsibility of the new church. By then a new minister, Alfred Pearson, had been in post at St Mark's for almost two years. He was a highly experienced parish priest, aged 48, who had previously ministered in Oxford, Nottingham, Leeds and Brighton. He brought his wife and six children, the youngest still a baby, to live at the vicarage in Melbourne Avenue. 'Quiet and retiring in manner',[31] Pearson was a thoughtful intellectual whose sermons were important enough to be published in a book entitled *The Claims of the Faith*.[32] They suggest that he was a powerful and eloquent preacher with a strong adherence to all the traditional doctrines of the church.

In his book *Fifty Years of Sheffield Church Life*, the well-known local clergyman, William Odom, described Pearson as a 'broad-minded evangelical'.[33] What did this mean? Odom's word picture of Anglican evangelicals in 1903 may be helpful:

17. The Revd Alfred Pearson (fourth from left) with members of the Men's Service and a dog.
The two curates, seated on chairs, were C.G. Lane and John Young.
We do not know which one is holding the cornet!

'sober, peaceable, and truly conscientious sons of the Church of England', deeply attached to her principles as propounded at the Reformation and embodied in the Book of Common Prayer .... We are here to affirm that it is not sufficient to worship God only, but that also it is of the utmost importance to worship Him rightly.[34]

This emphasis on liturgy and the Prayer Book suggests that the churchmanship of Odom and Pearson was more akin to that of mainstream Anglicans today than of modern Anglican Evangelicals. There is also greater confidence that worshipping 'rightly' will not be confused with the 'ritualism' so feared 20 years previously. By 1903, it no longer posed a major threat to the identity of the Anglican Church.

Like his predecessors, Pearson was a strong supporter of the Church Pastoral Aid Society, which raised funds to employ extra members of church staff, both ordained and lay. He was promoted to Rural Dean in 1900 and to a canonry of York in 1903. After eight years at St Mark's, he was appointed Suffragan Bishop of Burnley in 1904. The Bishop of Manchester had recommended him for the post, since he valued Pearson as a fellow-Evangelical who had worked in several 'large centres of industrial population'.[35] But Pearson did not serve long as a Bishop. He died in 1909.

The Mission Room

The congregation of St Mark's was scarcely typical of the industrial population of Sheffield or even of some parts of the parish. The Broomspring Lane area, in particular, was poor, with densely-populated back-to-back housing. Pearson actively tried to take the church to them by establishing a new mission room on Broomspring Lane. Although it opened after he left, it was his inspiration and

18. St Mark's Mission Room, opened Sunday 22 October 1905. This building was eventually sold to the City Council in 1979. It is still in use as the Broomhall Centre, a venue for a variety of community activities throughout the week. (Source: Picture Sheffield)

creation. The hall, which is still there, was 70 ft long and built of Crookes stone. It contained a large room that could seat 300 people, two classrooms and a kitchen. The aim was to provide services for local people 'who for some reason could not attend church'.[36]

One of these reasons would have been the pew rents, which were still levied at St Mark's and made poorer people feel excluded, even when open seats were available. Another was the style of service: the St Mark's clergy had heard that these people thought that 'certain services were above them and were not congregational enough: were too musical and not simple enough'. These musical services were the choir-led sung liturgy.

The solution proposed for the mission was a 'simple' evening service 'which they could all join in and the simplest could understand'. From October 1905, when the Mission Room opened, it became the particular responsibility of the senior curate. New societies and meetings were established, including the Mothers' Meeting and the Women's Bible Class. These were run by ladies who included the Misses Parkin and Miss Tozer, who hosted a summer garden party for members at her home on Hallam Gate Road. The Men's Service (previously held in the church) had attracted a congregation of 160 by 1907, when the curate C.G. Lane left St Mark's. He was clearly popular with 'the mission people', and they presented him with a Cyclostyle (an early form of duplicator) for his new parish. Lane joked that whenever his young son used the ink roller as make-up to play 'Red Indians' or 'The Wild Man of the Sea' he would think of them.[37]

Sunday schools, and a Band of Hope meeting for children every Monday evening, were held in the hall. The Anti-Drink campaign was a popular feature of the working-class mission in Victorian times, but by now some of its methods were seen as excessive. The curate emphasised that 'we carefully abstain from giving word-pictures of the drunken father turning his bare-footed and thinly-clad child into the snowy night'.[38] Half of the meeting time was allocated to craft activities, which may account for the average attendance of over 80.

The Bishop and St Mark's, 1905-11

The next phase of the history of St Mark's is unique. It may result from the church's prominence, its lucrative living or its desirable vicarage.[39] Whatever the reason, the incumbency was offered to the Suffragan Bishop of Sheffield, Dr John Edward Quirk. He was a graduate of St John's College, Cambridge, and his career had taken him to Yorkshire parishes, including Rotherham, and then to Bath, before he was appointed Vicar of Doncaster and Suffragan Bishop of Sheffield in 1901. This arrangement was terminated by the Archbishop of York, who felt that the Bishop needed a Sheffield parish, but Dr Quirk left Doncaster 'with the greatest possible regret'.[40]

At St Mark's, Dr Quirk quickly became popular for his 'energy, competence and general selflessness'.[41] The congregation accepted his part-time ministry and thought it 'a great success both for Sheffield and for St Mark's',[42] but Dr Quirk himself felt torn by his dual role. His dependence on the church staff caused acute anxiety when, for example, the vicar's warden announced he was leaving, or when both curates moved to new parishes at the same time.

On top of his other duties, Dr Quirk was aiding the Archbishop's efforts to establish a separate diocese, since Sheffield was still part of the enormous diocese of York. A Bishopric Committee was

19. The Rt Revd John Quirk, Suffragan Bishop of Sheffield and Vicar 1905-11.

set up in 1907 and a packed mass meeting in the Albert Hall[43] in November 1907 gave tremendous momentum to the campaign. Fund-raising reached £27,000 within a year, St Mark's naturally giving double the amount raised by any other church.[44] Success was dependent on support from the government, which finally passed the Bishopric Act in 1913. By then, Dr Quirk had given up the charge of St Mark's, although he remained a parishioner.

Many hoped that he would be elevated to the Bishop's throne, but Dr Quirk may have been too Evangelical for the taste of Cosmo Lang, the Archbishop of York.[45] The choice fell on a bishop from the southern province, Leonard Burrows, whose lack of experience of northern cities was much regretted in Sheffield. Dr Quirk himself behaved beautifully, presenting Dr Burrows at his investiture in the Cathedral.[46] He and his wife also donated the new Bishop's throne to the Cathedral. They left Sheffield shortly afterwards, when Dr Quirk was appointed Suffragan Bishop of Jarrow.

During Dr Quirk's ministry at St Mark's, the church was transformed by the introduction of electric lighting and the redecoration of the chancel. Sheffield's smoke, combined with gas lighting, had made the church quite dirty. A distinguished communion table was installed, in memory of Benjamin Burdekin, a churchwarden whose concerns over air pollution had led to the formation of the Sheffield Smoke Abatement Association. The vestry was transformed into a side chapel, apparently known as the 'Morning Chapel'.[47] New vestries for the clergy and choir were created on the other side of the chancel, next to the organ, which was enlarged and restored. Much of this expense was met once again by Colonel J.E. Cutler. A commemorative window in the chapel and a bronze memorial tablet were erected to this devoted supporter of St Mark's after his death in 1910.

Arthur Burnet Burney 1911-21

20. The new communion table in English oak, erected in 1907.[48]

21. The Revd Arthur Burnet Burney, Vicar 1911-21.

The next incumbent of St Mark's was almost the polar opposite of his predecessor, in being resolutely unambitious. Arthur Burnet Burney, who arrived in 1911, urged 'one claim' on his new congregation: 'that we who dwell at the Vicarage may be humbly allowed to enter into your common life and thought, that we may be made use of'. He valued above all 'the closeness of touch and real personal relationship between pastor and people'.[49] Burney had spent most of his previous ministry in Rotherham, describing his career as 'a Parochial Plodder in Poor Parishes'.[50] He found the task of adjusting to the congregation of St Mark's quite a challenge, as his Notes in the Parish Magazine show.[51]

Soon after his arrival, he had to contend with the 'exceedingly trying' loss of key members of staff, including both curates.[52] He was cheered by the arrival of his former Kimberworth curate, and Burney and his wife made it their first task to create a Sunday service for children and a branch of the Girls Friendly Society. This was held at the Parish Rooms, offered a range of enjoyable activities such as drama and dancing, and was a great success.[53] The highlight of the children's year was the Whit Sing, when singing to the assembled congregation from the terrace was followed by a picnic and games. In 1912, these were held in Fulwood and the children were conveyed using furniture vans: 'It is surprising how comfortable this kind of conveyance can be made and what a number of children can be stowed away in them.'[54] Presumably the 'vans' were large carts!

22: Sunday School outing to Wharncliffe at Whitsuntide, probably 1911.
(Picture courtesy of Andrew Braybrook)

Arthur Burney led St Mark's through the terrible war years, supported the young men who left on active service and grieved with the parents of those who did not return. Forty-three names were inscribed on the Memorial Tablet erected on the west wall in 1920, including the son of Mr and Mrs H.P. Marsh. Another son had died just before the war. Both H.P. Marsh and his father were church wardens and the lives of the Marsh brothers were commemorated in a window in the side chapel depicting the Resurrection. The verger, Charles George Powell, died in 1916 having served St Mark's since 1870 – a total of 46 years, spanning the entire history of the stone church. His unparalleled dedication to the church was celebrated in the erection of a brass tablet to his memory.

23 and 24: Plan for the First World War Memorial tablet showing the original surround in Irish Green Marble (Sheffield Archives Dioc/FAC/195) and the 'Latin Metal' tablet now in north east porch.

In the final year of the war, Burney established the Guild of St Mark as a focus for the congregation, especially its young people. Monthly Guild services were held, as well as social activities, which included drama, fancy dress and garden parties. The Guild had a serious purpose – 'to bind us more closely together in communion with CHRIST and one another'. It aimed to encourage its members to attend communion regularly, study the Bible and 'witness loyally for GOD and against sin'. The Guild became a permanent feature of St Mark's, supporting the church and its people in the difficult years to come.

25. The Rules of the Guild of St Mark's.

26. A typical Parish Magazine cover in the years 1907-20.

Notes

Jubilee History = *St Mark's Church, Broomhall, 1871 to 1921*, ed Arthur B. Burney (Sheffield: Northend, 1921).

NCS = Newspaper Cuttings relating to Sheffield (in Sheffield Central Library 942.74 SF/SQ).

[1] 'The Preachers of Sheffield: Their Churches and People by Criticus. No XXXVII St Mark's Church', *Sheffield Post*, 26 July 1873 [henceforward Criticus 1873].

[2] 'Death of the Revd W. Milton', obituary notice, NCS, Vol. 13, p. 158 (SF).

[3] *Sheffield Daily Telegraph*, 20 March 1867.

[4] Milton pays tribute to his help in 'Address to the congregation of St Mark's, Broomhall, Sheffield 1881-2', pp. 8-9. Sheffield Local Studies Library. Ref Vol 10, No 18, J 042S.

[5] Criticus 1873.

[6] Criticus 1873.

[7] Criticus 1873.

[8] Jubilee History, p. 8.

[9] StMark's Mutual Improvement Association, *Annual Report, 1888-9,* and *1889-90.*

[10] St Mark's Mutual Improvement Association, Programme, 17 and 18 February 1890.

[11] Milton, 'Address to the congregation', p. 6.

[12] Milton, 'Address to the congregation', p. 4. He speaks of 'the ravages of the Great Destroyer which have carried away so many of the Congregation of St. Mark's as a flood'. Marsh died suddenly aged 55 in November 1881 and Rodgers followed in April 1882, but there is no evidence of a dramatic 'flood' of deaths.

[13] Report of William Milton's funeral, NCS, Vol. 1, p. 85 (SQ).

[14] Criticus 1873.

[15] E.R. Wickham, *Church and People in an Industrial City* (London: Lutterworth, 1957), Appendix 1, p. 275: only 35 seats were set aside for the poor, p.144.

[16] *Sheffield and Rotherham Independent*, 17 December 1883.

[17] William Odom, *Hallamshire Worthies: Characteristics and Work of Notable Sheffield Men and Women* (Sheffield: J.H. Northend and Sons, 1926), p.45; J.H. Stainton, *The Making of Sheffield 1865-1914* (Sheffield: E. Weston and Sons, 1924), pp. 305-6.

[18] Odom, *Hallamshire Worthies*, pp. 44-5.

[19] 'In Memoriam, Henry Arnold Favell', 25 September 1896 in William Odom, *Sheffield Church Notes*, Vol. 1 (SCL 283.4271S).

[20] Odom, *Hallamshire Worthies,* p. 45.

[21] *S. Mark's Parish Magazine*, May 1940.

[22] William Odom, *Fifty Years of Sheffield Church Life 1866-1916* (Sheffield: Northend, 1917), p. 112.

[23] *S. Mark's Parish Magazine*, May 1940.

[24] Stainton, *The Making of Sheffield*, pp. 280-1; Odom, *Sheffield Church Notes*, Vol. 1 August 1893.

[25] The obituary in Odom, *Hallamshire Worthies*, pp. 45, describes it as 'an insidious disease'. The Jubilee History p. 13, describes it as 'a short and painful illness', but this could have been the final stage.

[26] Odom, *Hallamshire Worthies*, p. 46. Odom's comment is strikingly prescient in view of the survival of St Augustine's and destruction of St Mark's.

[27] This account of the building of St Augustine's is taken from William Odom, *Memorials of Sheffield* (Sheffield: Northend, 1922), pp. 205-8; see also F.L. Preston, 'A guide to St Augustine's Church, Endcliffe, Sheffield', unpublished typescript.

[28] Odom, *Hallamshire Worthies*, p. 46.

[29] Jubilee History, p. 16.

[30] Preston, 'Guide to St Augustine's Church', p. 1.

[31] Odom, *Fifty Years of Sheffield Church Life*, p. 107.

[32] Alfred Pearson, *The Claims of the Faith on the Practice of To-day* (London: James Nisbet, 1905).

[33] Odom, *Fifty Years of Sheffield Church Life*, p. 107

[34] Odom, *Fifty Years of Sheffield Church Life*, pp. 151-2 (quoting his own speech in 1903).

[35] 'New Bishop Suffragan of Burnley', *The Times*, 3 January 1905.

[36] 'St Mark's Mission Room. Dedication Service', *Sheffield Daily Independent*, 23 October 1905. The following quotations are also taken from this account.

[37] *S. Mark's Parish Magazine*, September 1907.

[38] *S. Mark's Parish Magazine*, April 1912.

[39] 'New Vicar of St Mark's. Bishop of Sheffield accepts the Living', *Sheffield Daily Independent*, 6 February 1905, states that the income from the living of St Mark's was £630; Doncaster's was £495 and Quirk's previous Rotherham church yielded only £300.

[40] 'New Vicar of St Mark's. Bishop of Sheffield accepts the Living', *Sheffield Daily Independent*, 6 February 1905.

[41] Mary Walton, *A History of the Diocese of Sheffield 1914-1949* (Sheffield: Diocesan Board of Finance, 1981), p. 4.

[42] H.P. Marsh speaking at the Easter Vestry meeting in 1906, *Sheffield Daily Independent*, 20 April 1906.

[43] The Albert Hall was in Barker's Pool on the site of the current John Lewis store. It burned down in 1937.

[44] 'St Mark's. A Year of Exceptional Expenditure', *Sheffield Daily Independent*, 24 April 1908. At least two members of the St Mark's congregation held senior roles on the Committee – H.P. Marsh and H.B. Sandford. See Walton, *History of the Diocese of Sheffield*, pp. 4-5.

[45] This is the suggestion of Mary Walton (*History of the Diocese of Sheffield*, p.17).

[46] Walton, *History of the Diocese of Sheffield*, p. 18.

[47] William Odom: *Memorials of Sheffield*, pp. 179-81.

[48] *S. Mark's Parish Magazine*, February 1907

[49] *S. Mark's Parish Magazine,* October 1912.

[50] *S. Mark's Parish Magazine,* January 1912.

[51] The monthly Parish Magazines have been preserved from January 1911, with a gap during World War I.

[52] *S. Mark's Parish Magazine*, May 1911.

[53] Interview with Margaret Braybrook on 21 June 2012.

[54] *S. Mark's Parish Magazine,* June 1912.

27. The nave and chancel, probably in the inter-war years.

CHAPTER 3

THE INTER-WAR YEARS

Tim Moore

'In 50 years, times and methods of Church finance have changed… It is well that Church Councils, with statutory powers, should come to the rescue and spread the responsibility. For S.Mark's, as with all, the value of money is at least halved; time and means of locomotion have wrought sad changes in our congregation and parish. There are two things that have not changed, the one God above us all, and the spirit of loving loyalty in you all.'
The Revd A.B. Burney, 1921[1]

Setting up the PCC

At 8pm on 16 April 1920, a meeting was held in the Ashgate Road Rooms – a gathering of the great and the good of St Mark's: Mr Green; Mr Marsh; Mr J.D. Hill; 'Pa' Kelk, the Scoutmaster; Commander Jackson; one of the Parkin sisters, Helen; and Miss Fanny Louisa Tozer of the Tozer steel family. The Wardens, H.M. Elliott and J.D. Webster, already had an official role to play in proceedings, as did the Vicar, who opened with a prayer, then requested nominations for the first Lay Vice-Chair of the first Parochial Church Council of St Mark's.

The route to this moment had started with the Church of England's frustration at being run by parliament. In 1916, the archbishops had set up a committee on Church and State to look into alternatives. The chairman, Lord Selborne, recommended the establishment of a Church Assembly. The Archbishop of Canterbury, Randall Davidson, knew that such legislation would not be passed in wartime, but William Temple, leader of the 'Life and Liberty' movement – who said, at the Queens Hall in 1917: 'We demand freedom for the Church of England' – sought to force it through. Consequently, the resulting Enabling Act of 1919 was a watered-down version of the committee's proposals, allowing for the setting up of a Church Assembly of 95 lay members to carry out part of the role hitherto played by parliament.[2] The Parochial Church Councils were a local element of this, designed to remove much of the administrative burden from the clergy and to democratise the vestry meetings that had been seen by some as run by a select cabal who determined parish affairs behind closed doors.

In *S.Mark's Parish Magazine* for January 1920, the Revd Burney described the Act as putting the church 'on trial' and said that the church must 'save herself'[3]. He issued a rallying call to get people out into the parish and muster up names to go on the electoral roll. Members of the congregation were encouraged to go door to door, signing up anyone who was over 18 and not a declared member of another religion. In February he wrote:

> If you feel the church is asleep or ... out of touch ... out of date ... then now is the time for you to ... wake us up ... throw in your lot with those that believe a reformed church has a live part to play in the rebuilding of our national life.[4]

This suggests that Burney, at least, linked the reform of the Enabling Act with the wider reconstruction following World War I.

By March, Burney conceded that 'more interest will be shown when more people understand the

Parish Councils[15]. By April, the Electoral Roll had gathered more than 1,000 names and was pinned, Martin Luther-like, to the church door. The first parochial meeting was set for 16 April; it would elect the members of the PCC, who had to be over 21, communicants and seconded. Burney wrote that the PCC should be responsible for all 'progressive', as well as financial, matters.[6]

The minutes of that meeting are written in the elegant copperplate hand of Mr E. Hayward, who had either been elected to, or assumed, the role of secretary. Mr E. Benson proposed Mr Burbridge for Lay Vice-Chair, seconded by Mr B.H. Hoole. Mr Burbridge was unwilling to be put forward, either from genuine humility or from reluctance to take on the burden, but the Council elected him anyway, and he humbly accepted.

The first two decisions taken by the newly-formed PCC typified the work that they were to do. Mr Rodgers, the church organist, had recently died and a subcommittee was formed to find a replacement. This was the first of many committees. They also debated how to raise the £200 (£8,120 in today's money) for the Diocesan Quota. Burney suggested a levy on every communicant. Mr Hallam proposed one shilling a week from everyone on the electoral list. In the end they put up the pew rents by 50%, to 10s 6d, which was announced at the next meeting on 4 October, the day before the wedding of the curate, the Revd John Garfield Roberts.

He had met Miss Erica Nelson Walsh while working in the parish, and went on a motorbike-and-sidecar touring holiday with her in July 1920. On 5 October, they married and moved across Sheffield to Brightside, where he took up the parish of St Margaret's. Roberts would go on to a parish in Stocksbridge and was with their scout troop when it lit the hilltop coronation beacon for King George VI in 1937.

The 1921 Jubilee and the Revd Mannering

In 1921, the 50th anniversary of the consecration of the church was celebrated with a Jubilee week of special services, and the production of a booklet detailing the church's 50-year history. The Jubilee was planned in the autumn of 1920, when Burney also complained that he was in financial straits, and appealed to the PCC for permission to either sell the vicarage or rent the top floor as a flat, or else to give him the Easter offerings. The Council opted instead to increase his stipend – with help from the Easter Offerings – by 50% to £600. Burney told them 'not to consider it as finally settled'[7]. In March 1921, the Jubilee collection found a worthy cause when the church wardens called attention to the large audiences at the Ashgate Road Rooms, the poor provision for escape, and the danger 'which would be incurred in case of panic'.[8] An idea from an anonymous member of the Council that the Jubilee effort be used to attract a larger regular congregation, was not seconded. Instead, it was proposed that the collection should go towards the 'reconstruction' of the Ashgate Road Rooms. The motion was carried by a vote of 12 to 3, with Mr Gray appointed to oversee the project, as it was a 'very grave consideration and a big thing for the council to undertake'.[9]

Mr E.T. Northend, owner of J.W. Northend Ltd, the printers of *S.Mark's Parish Magazine*, produced the Jubilee booklet free of charge, the proceeds going to the Jubilee fund. The booklet was bound in thick, textured paper, with the lion of St Mark's on the cover, in the centre of a Celtic-style cross with a patterned border. Inside, the jubilee week services were listed, followed by a history of St Mark's written by the Vicar, listing all the incumbents, along with their photographs. Either because Burney drew most of his history from the accounts books, or because of his own preoccupation with financial matters, the booklet gave excessive emphasis to the fiscal history of the church.

Although detailing extensive charity giving, Burney also feared that the parish could not continue with such large maintenance costs: 'we shall only maintain our proud position by "each rowing his or her weight in the boat," from oldest to youngest.' His mission, while Vicar, had been to 'eas[e] the upkeep of the place in time to come'.[10]

When the curate, John Garfield Roberts, left, Burney initially thought that Roberts' brother, Ivor, would come in to fill the gap. This fell through, however, possibly because Ivor became ill over Christmas 1920, and Burney panicked about carrying Christmas on his own. In April 1921, the Revd John Wallace Gleave was appointed to the parish as curate. He had received a 1st class degree in theology in 1912 from St John's College, Cambridge, where he won several prizes, including one for understanding of the Greek Testament. He was ordained priest in 1914 on the Isle of Man while Vice-Principal of the Bishop Wilson Theology College, and rose to be Principal the following year.

28. The Revd John Wallace Gleave, Curate, 1921-24, and Vicar, 1931-59.

During World War I, Gleave, like most clergy, was made a Temporary Chaplain to the Forces. The Isle of Man had two alien civilian internment camps and it is likely that Gleave became involved with these camps, especially the one at Knockaloe, near Peel, since this was close to the college at Bishopscourt.

At a PCC meeting on Friday, 22 April 1921, two days before the start of the Jubilee services, Burney announced his retirement from St Mark's, citing the need for someone new to take over, and for them to reach more people in the parish, 'particularly now when the burden of finance was so much heavier'[11]. He was taking over as Rector of Alford with Hornblotton in Somersetshire, stating that his wife's health required the warmer weather. He would stay there until 1935, when he became Vicar at Dunster, being promoted to Prebendary and Canon of Henstridge in Wells Cathedral in 1936. He died on 16 February 1956, at the age of 87, and was remembered in St Mark's for his work with the Guild of St Mark's (see page 26). His stated aim was to have at least 100 communicants at every 8am service.

The Jubilee week started on Sunday, 24 April 1921, with the Bishop of Sheffield, the Right Revd Leonard Burrows, preaching at the 11am service. The collections for that Sunday's services went towards what was described as the 'Reconstruction of the Parish Rooms'. On Wednesday, 27 April, the Archdeacon of Sheffield, Charles Lisle Carr, preached at the 8pm Evensong. On the following Sunday, 1 May, there were four services, with Burney's predecessor, the Right Revd John Nathaniel Quirk, now Bishop of Jarrow, returning to preach at the 11am service.

In October 1921, the Revd Ernest Mannering arrived to take over as incumbent, leaving his posts as both Vice-Principal at St Aidan's Theology College in Birkenhead and teacher of Hellenistic Greek at the University of Liverpool. Mannering had spent his curacy at Holy Trinity, Marylebone, and had then been a vicar in Woking. After this, he was appointed to the Bishop Wilson College on the Isle of Man in 1913, at the same time as Gleave. It is inconceivable that the two men had not known each other, particularly as they both became Principal, as well as carrying out chaplaincy work for the forces. Whether Mannering was appointed to St Mark's on a recommendation from Gleave, or whether it was a happy coincidence, we do not know.

29. The Revd Ernest Mannering,
Vicar 1921–31.

30 Mrs Irene Mannering.
This photograph was inscribed
'Bible Class 1930'.

The Sports Field

Despite Burney's desire that St Mark's scale back any extension plans and consolidate its financial position in case the outlook should become bleak, a considerable amount of money was still spent by the PCC.

The Sports Field on Coldwell Lane, Crosspool, which had been bought in May 1920 for £680 (some £8,000 in today's money) by the St Mark's Communicants Guild and Comrades of the Great War, required physical and financial investment, since it was really just uneven scrubland at the time of its purchase. A cricket pitch was laid first, and then tennis courts and a football pitch were marked out. The field was officially opened on 21 July 1923.

It was a good investment: many people had fond memories of the Sports Field. Ray Holehouse, who was born in Broomhill, recalled there being two cricket teams and two football teams. Margaret Braybrook (nee Wardlow) remembers that her older brother, Ted, played regularly for one of the football teams in the '20s, and sulked at teatime whenever they lost.[12]

31. Margaret Braybrook (nee Wardlow)
(fourth from right) with friends on a
Sunday school outing in 1919.

In the mid '20s, Margaret and her siblings would go to the field for the Whitsuntide sports days, held after the unofficial Whit Sing on the fields of King Edward VII School. Her father would go for a pint after the singing, and then take her and the other children to the sports field, where they would be immediately presented with paper bags of sandwiches and buns. There were all kinds of races on the field – egg-and-spoon, sprinting, and sack races – as well as many other games, followed, at the end of the day, by prize-giving and refreshments of home-baked cake, provided by the ladies of the congregation. In April 1923, Gleave presented plans to the Church Council for a pavilion in which to serve refreshments. When built, it was insured for £130.

In 1927, the Sports Field Committee petitioned the PCC for £100 to lay a hard tennis court, saying that they lost members – and therefore revenue – because of bad weather. The Council initially refused the loan since, they argued, there was no security to be put against it. It was eventually granted when the Committee raised part of the amount themselves.

In December 1931, plans were accepted for a kitchen in the pavilion. They were put forward by the Mothers' Union, who had provided refreshments there for years. A year later, two additional sub-committees were formed for the pavilion, one for security, the other a 'Ladies Refreshment Committee'. In 1933, during the economic depression, sanction was given for the sports field to be used by groups of the unemployed.

Financial Developments and Renovations

By June 1923, Mannering had evidently tasted the same financial problems encountered by Burney and he got the permission of the Church Burgesses to sell the vicarage on Melbourne Avenue and to buy the (relatively) smaller property at 4 St Mark's Crescent. At a PCC meeting in February 1926, Mr P. Marsh announced that he was unhappy about the sale of the old vicarage, since the new one was, he felt, far too small for a parish such as St Mark's.

32. The present St Mark's Vicarage, 4 St Mark's Crescent, purchased in 1924.

It was not until May 1924 that the Ashgate Road Reconstruction Committee decided what work needed to be done to improve the parish rooms. The list included: installing two 'sunlight' gas stoves to solve the heating problem; decorating, painting and cleaning; turning the small upstairs room into a ladies lavatory; and building a headquarters for St Mark's Scouts, for whom it was decided to build a brick hut with a sloping roof in one of the yards. One estimate for the painting came to £95 10s, while installing a toilet came to £80. The PCC stipulated that the money for the scout hut was to be raised by the scouts, not the church.

Late in 1924, the Revd Gleave left to be Succentor of Coventry Cathedral. The ladies of St Mark's put on a much-praised farewell luncheon for him. He would remain in Coventry until 1927, when he would become Vicar of St Paul's in Walsall. St Mark's would be without a curate for several years, saving the parish money and earning Mannering praise for carrying the work on his own.

On 18 May 1926, the PCC met to consider an architect's report on the church. The vicar had found that no maintenance work had been undertaken for 20 years and had called for the report to be made. It recommended that treatment be carried out on exterior walls, new paths laid, and wire guards fitted to protect the windows. Inside, the heating system required new boilers and new grates, and the walls were recommended to be painted a warm, yellow-cream colour. The costs were estimated at £1,800, with £150 on top of that for new heating in the Ashgate Rooms, since the 'sunlight' stoves had been heavily criticised.

The church was closed from the beginning of August to 10 October for the work to be completed, and the Revd Canon Grose Hodge giving the first sermon in the renovated church. The total cost of renovations was actually closer to £2,000, with nearly £522 coming from Miss Thomas's Bequest, made at the end of 1919 for the fabric of the church.

On 18 December 1927, the Revd Douglass Hopkins was appointed as the new curate. An English Literature graduate of Keble College, Oxford, he gained his theology diploma in 1926, only becoming a deacon in the same year as he joined St Mark's. At his ordination, a processional cross was used, much to the annoyance of Mr Hill, who stated that this 'laid us open to the danger of the cross being looked upon as an object of adoration and paved the way for an increase in ceremonialism'.[13] His formal objection at the PCC was defeated by a vote of 16 to 1. Hopkins was a keen actor and became involved in the Lent plays put on by Miss Helen Parkin, which had been an institution since 1920 and continued until 1939. Mrs Marjorie Wilcockson remembered them as 'the social event of the year', and that to be involved required a form of apprenticeship, moving up through the ranks from serving tea and biscuits, selling programmes, etc., until you were finally allowed into the cast. One play involving Mr Hopkins, whom Mrs Wilcockson described as 'very handsome and caused a great flutter amongst the younger ladies', required him to kiss a 'pert' French maid.[14] It was somehow decided that it would be more suitable for the maid to be played by a married woman.

Douglass Hopkins is also remembered as being a very good minister, taking great care with his pastoral work. When Margaret Braybrook's elder sister, Edith, was hit by a car in 1929, Hopkins spent time with her. He gave the badly injured woman a New Testament, writing in an accompanying letter:

> Here is the little Testament which I promised you. It is only small, as I said, but it is light to hold, and I hope it will be always a source of help and comfort to you. God has so often spoken to me out of its pages, that I know how much strength and help can be derived from reading it. May it

33 and 34. A Mothers' Union garden party in the 1920s. In both pictures, Miss Tozer is in the front row, second from the left. In the left-hand picture, Douglass Hopkins is the curate on the back row.

35.Women of St Mark's, with the Curate, Douglass Hopkins, back left and Miss Tozer second from the right at the front.

be a great blessing to you Edith. It will be a joy to me always to know that you are reading it each day.[15]

Edith died of her injuries in 1930.

The financial situation continued to present difficulties. In May 1928, Mannering described the condition of the church organ as 'in the habit of issuing distressing noises at inconvenient times'.[16] A maintenance check in March 1929 found that the stops were clogged with dirt and the engine needed replacing; the necessary work would cost over £1,000. The Broomspring Lane Mission Hall, where Margaret Braybrook took Sunday School lessons under both Helen and Mary Parkin, also required repairs, which would cost £350. And, at the PCC meeting of November 1929, it was announced that the drains in St Mark's Crescent had been condemned by the City Council and would require at least £100 to fix. Far from becoming a prudent church, as Burney had wanted, St Mark's instead found spending hard to avoid.

Following the Stock Market crash of 1929, Britain's economy took a nose dive; the numbers of unemployed rose from 1 million before the crash to 3 million by 1931 and exports fell by 50%. The economic difficulties were especially keenly felt in industrial and coal mining areas, such as South Yorkshire. Unemployment in some areas of the north reached 70%. In 1935, some tens of thousands of Sheffield workers fought a three-hour battle with police outside City Hall, when they gathered to call for a living wage. St Mark's response to this economic crisis seems to have been negligible. In 1920, giving to the 'Poor and Parochial' fund was often coupled with giving for Church Expenses, the former being allocated around 5% of the combined offerings. By 1931, this had gone up to around 20%. There is no documented appeal to assist with the economic depression, other than clerical expressions of despair at the national situation. The church's attention was instead focused on supporting missionary work abroad, with giving and dedicated offerings for the work of the Church Missionary Society, an evangelical organisation that raised huge sums of money to support its foreign missionaries. For many years, St Mark's had its own missionary, whom the church supported financially. The missionary would send letters to St Mark's and preach the occasional sermon when on furlough in England.

The 1932 Fire in the Ashgate Road Rooms

In the early hours of 15 April 1932, the Ashgate Road Rooms were completely gutted by fire. The crews of the two fire engines sent to the scene called for reinforcements before they even arrived at the blaze, since, at 1am, they could see the bright glare glowing in the neighbourhood. When they arrived, flames were licking upwards from the windows and part of the roof. It only took the firemen half an hour to bring the fire under control, but they left a contingent to work there all night. The roof completely fell in at one point, nearly killing the firemen in the hall. Even the heavy stone of the walls was charred and cracked by the fierce heat. The panelled walls and the pitch pine covering the ceiling, along with the wooden chairs and props from a performance by the Girls Friendly Society the night before, were all perfect fuel for a vicious fire. The *Yorkshire Telegraph and Star*, then printed as one newspaper, stated that the fire had been caused either by a match or a cigarette possibly dropped by one of the 200 people in the audience earlier, or by an electrical fault, also connected with the performance.

The previous year had already been one of change for St Mark's. The Revd Mannering departed for St Peter's, Brockley. A farewell party and presentation was held for him and his wife on 29

36. The aftermath of the fire at the Parish Rooms.
(Source: *Yorkshire Telegraph and Star*, **15 April, 1932**).

December 1930. He would go on to serve as Rural Dean in Wadhurst diocese, Chichester, from 1935. The Revd Gleave returned, this time as Vicar, being inducted on 14 April 1931. Then, in December, the Revd Douglass Hopkins left to become Vicar at Holy Trinity, Millhouses; he remained there until 1940, when he became a chaplain with the Royal Navy, serving until 1946. St Mark's raised £72 as a farewell gift for him. Gleave secured Arthur King as curate, a theology graduate of St John's College, Durham, and winner of the Vul Hebrew Prize in 1930. He was appointed on 22 May 1932, being made Deacon in the parish on his birthday.[17]

Arthur King had been a boarder at King Edward VII school, across the road from St Mark's, and remembered running through the streets of the parish on cross-country runs, and at other times parading through them, rifle on shoulder, following the school's Officer Training Corps drum and fife band. He was encouraged to undertake as many activities as possible, one of which was to assist with the choir boys' outings, usually to Southport. Describing his duties on the train, he said he had 'to time each boy's turn aloft in the luggage rack and to referee their boxing matches [...] there was never a dull moment.'[18]

King described the parish as generous and said that they gave comparatively freely for Hospital Sunday and the Church's own missionary, Dr J.A. Martin of the Church Missionary Society. He also recalled being fed well – and to excess, even during the depression when there were mass lay-offs in the steel industry, even among the managerial class living near the church.[19]

By this time Gleave was at his peak, a skilled orator who was often asked to repeat his sermons. His churchmanship leant towards a broad-minded evangelicalism. In October 1937, Gleave's theology was such that he wished to change the wording of the fourth commandment as it was read in the church. He explained that, in light of the knowledge mankind had of the gradual development of the earth, he had reservations about using the 'for in six days' portion of the commandment and wished to omit it. The PCC agreed, with two dissenters.[20] Services at St Mark's required great eloquence since that was virtually the only concession to aesthetic appeal that was permitted: a certain lady in the congregation, whom King declined to identify, refused even to allow candles on the altar. Gleave was for a long time Honorary Secretary of the Diocesan Conference, and propelled his raw curate into being Diocesan Inspector of Church Day Schools. King, being skilled in biblical languages, also taught Hellenistic Greek to two university students as well as to the Vicar's son, John. His knowledge of Hebrew allowed him to discuss Jewish scriptures and faith with a Jewish household. His teaching duties also extended to taking the sixth form at Rotherham Girls High School for the Archbishop's Diploma in Religious Knowledge.

Margaret Braybrook took her first communion on Parish Sunday on 22 March 1931. The Prayer Book given to her was signed by Deaconess Gertrude Western, whom she knew well. Margaret joined the Girls' Friendly Society, which taught dance and choral pieces. These were performed in competitions, and the St Mark's group were successful: in 1930, the Members' Choir won the Diocesan Competition for the third year running and the dance team came a narrow second.

Margaret remembers travelling to Leeds and Barnsley for other competitions, the group wearing dresses made especially for the performance.

After the fire, a committee, inevitably, was formed to rebuild the Church Rooms. By June, the Ashgate Rooms Reconstruction Committee had received the insurance payout of £1,688 (after the £42 claims assessor fees were paid) and Mr Edgar Northend sketched out plans for a 'large hall on the ground floor together with a new kitchen and lavatories, and retaining the present frontage of the building with provision upstairs for classrooms'[21]. The architect, Mr J.P. Hunter, was engaged, and estimated the costs at £3,000, leaving £1,300 to be raised, and a further £500 for furnishing. The Church Rooms were not simply to be restored, the PCC was told; they were to be redesigned for a new era.

In September 1932, the Reconstruction Committee employed W. Marlow and Sons to build the Parish Hall for £3,643. Fundraising had, by then, accumulated the first £1,000 of the amount needed. A flaw in the plans required them to draw up a formal agreement with Mr Ernest Osborne of 499 Glossop Road to allow the metal ladder escape hatch to 'land' in his grounds, for which he was to be paid 1 shilling per annum by the PCC.

During building, wood panelling was added in all the classrooms to a height of 3 feet, but it was decided, for reasons of cost, not to introduce running hot water to the kitchen and lavatories. Decorating the hall with panelling on the staircase, distempering, varnishing and furnishing – including 100 folding chairs, 150 normal chairs, stage apparatus and folding card tables – rumbled on until 1935, and encountered several faults in the construction, such as the accumulation of water in the cellar and under the stage.

The Hall was officially opened on 22 April 1933 by Miss Fanny Louisa Tozer, since she had loaned the church £1,500 so that the work could be finished. Coming from a wealthy steel family, Miss Tozer was a prominent member of the St Mark's community, frequently holding garden parties at her house on Hallamgate Road. In addition to her generosity to St Mark's, the 1947 guide to

37. The Parish Hall in Ashgate Road, reconstructed after the 1932 fire. After the bombing of the church in 1940, the Hall was used for services for more than 20 years. Around 1969, it was sold to Sheffield City Council as a library store. It is now a block of student flats.

38. Miss Tozer, daughter of steel magnate, Edward Tozer.

Sheffield Cathedral says: 'The Chapter House....will forever be one of the treasures of the Cathedral...In its entirety it is the gift of Miss [F.L] Tozer, her memorial to her father and mother.' Her father, Edward Tozer, was from 1875 a Director of Steel, Peach and Tozer, one of the biggest steel companies in Sheffield and Rotherham. The St Mark's Parish Hall was ceremoniously unlocked with a special key handed over by the architect. A newspaper account described the hall as 'excellently designed, to which many modern improvements have been added'. It was dedicated to Gleave and was said to be 'perhaps the best parish hall in Sheffield'.[22]

The effort and imagination put into rebuilding the hall would come to sustain the church, keeping it alive during and after the war. But it would also ultimately delay the rebuilding of St Mark's, since there were other parishes in the diocese worse off from the bombing.

The Eve of Destruction

In 1938, the Revd Arthur King married and left the parish for Thurcroft Conventional district. This was a mining community and the church there was in the process of being built. In 1942, King became Rector of Bradfield, also taking on Sheffield Diocese Youth Council until 1945, then editing the Diocese Year Book. The Revd Arnold Birkett Swallow, another former pupil of King Edward VII School, was appointed in King's place in 1938. A Cambridge classics graduate, Swallow went to theological college 12 years after leaving university.

In March 1938, plans were started for the installation of a new stained glass window, paid for by Mrs S.G. Brown of London in memory of her aunt, Mrs Jowitt, who had worshipped at St Mark's for 45 years and had died on 29 December 1937. By September, Mrs Brown had approved a design depicting the raising of the widow's son at Nain. The new window was described as being of three panels, the first 'He went into the city', the second 'There was a dead man carried out', and the third 'He sat up and began to speak'. Above them were the heraldic symbols of the thistle and lion of Scotland and the St Andrew's cross. It was dedicated on 7 May 1940, only to be destroyed just seven months later when the church was bombed.

In a series of articles in the Parish Magazine, all of the church's stained glass windows were described and explained (see Appendix 3). One of the last descriptions, in September 1940, is of those in the chapel, including one depicting an Easter scene of angels and the women at the tomb. It was dedicated to Harry Evelyn Marsh, who had died in 1914, and John Lockwood Marsh, Captain, 114th Battalion, York and Lancaster Regiment, who had died in action on 16 October 1915.

After the outbreak of World War II, Gleave, who had been made an Honorary Canon of St Matthew in Sheffield Cathedral in 1939, wrote several times on the war in *S Mark's Parish Magazine*. In May 1940, the 'Vicar's Note' says that peace was impossible while 'brutal and aggressive powers that have no regard for truth and honour' existed in the world. The last seven months, he says, have torn away the veil which hides so many things in international relations [...] we can see to what depths man can sink when he rejects God.' He ends this letter by saying that there can be 'no patched up peace [...] German and the allied; one or the other must be destroyed.'[23]

In June, Gleave writes of a 'spiritual conflict'. He goes on to say: 'We are fighting to save not only our Country and Empire, but also the right to act and speak and worship as free men.' News of the '[i]nhuman methods of warfare' in Holland and Belgium had reached him, and he rejected the idea that the British spirit could be broken through possible similar atrocities:

The bombing of women and children in this country, so far from intimidating us, would make every Briton so savage in his hatred of German brutality that he would never lay down his arms until the evil thing had been completely destroyed, not if the war went on for thirty years![24]

The bombing of British military mainland targets did not start until July. Civilian targets were not hit until 7 September.

It is unlikely that Gleave's articles were anything other than opinion pieces, reflecting his keen interest in international affairs, rather than a form of news dissemination. In 1938, four out of every five homes in Britain had a radio and the events of the war would have been followed closely.

On an average Sunday early in 1940, the church would have been occupied by a cast of regular characters.[25] The first six rows on the left side in front of the pulpit were almost completely booked up. In the third row were the two seats of the Misses Helen and Mary Parkin, beside Mr and Mrs Henderson, and in front of Mrs Brailsford, who had been coming to the church since the earliest days and remembered horse-drawn carriages queuing on the crescent. On the right side, four rows back, sat Capt. Wilkinson in a single seat beside a pillar. He was a retired naval officer who would always command 'As you were!' whenever he made a slip of the tongue while reading morning lessons.[26] In the row behind him was the vicarage pew, where Mrs Gleave would sit with the two teenage children and watch her husband preach from the pulpit. On the far left, two thirds of the way to the back was the entire row reserved for Mr E.T. Northend, proprietor of J.W. Northend printing, an upstanding member, and former Secretary, of the PCC.

In April 1940, during the penultimate PCC meeting before the church was bombed, a portentous event was described. 'An imbecile boy gained access to the [Parish Hall] and lit a fire on the stage.'[27] Two rover scouts discovered the fire and dealt with it. It was estimated that repairs and redecoration would cost £32. The scouts, at the time, can have had no idea that, by stopping the fire, they were saving the St Mark's community, which would surely have disintegrated without the Parish Hall during the long years after the bombing that December.

39. The boys of St Mark's choir in the 1930s.

40. Aerial view of the old St Mark's church building.

Notes

[1] Jubilee History, *St Mark's Church 1871–1921* (Sheffield: J.W. Northend Publishing, 1921), pp. 21-2.

[2] A. Hastings, *History of English Christianity 1920-1985* (London: Fount, 1987), pp. 62-3. In 1970, the Church Assembly changed its name to the General Synod.

[3] *S. Mark's Parish Magazine*, January 1920.

[4] *S. Mark's Parish Magazine*, February 1920.

[5] *S. Mark's Parish Magazine*, March 1920.

[6] *S. Mark's Parish Magazine*, April 1920.

[7] Minutes of St Mark's PCC, 6 December 1920.

[8] Minutes of St Mark's PCC, 4 March 1921.

[9] Minutes of St Mark's PCC, 4 March 1921.

[10] *St Mark's Church 1871–1921*, p. 22.

[11] Minutes of St Mark's PCC, 22 April 1921.

[12] Margaret Braybrook, interviewed 21 June 2012, and accompanying notes of memories compiled by Andrew Braybrook, 20 June 2012.

[13] Minutes of St Mark's PCC, 12 December 1927.

[14] 'Mistress Wilcockson's Tale' in *S. Mark's Parish Magazine*, June 1990.

[15] Margaret Braybrook, interviewed 21 June 2012, and accompanying notes of memories, including the letter enclosed with the prayerbook, compiled by Andrew Braybrook, 20 June 2012.

[16] Minutes of St Mark's PCC, 8 May 1928.

[17] *Crockford's Clerical Directory* (London: Church House Publishing, 1940)

[18] *S. Mark's Parish Magazine*, March 1971.

[19] *S. Mark's Parish Magazine*, March 1971.

[20] Minutes of St Mark's PCC, 28 October 1937.

[21] Minutes of St Mark's PCC, 8 June 1932.

[22] *Yorkshire Telegraph and Star*, 24 April 1933.

[23] *S. Mark's Parish Magazine*, May 1940/

[24] *S. Mark's Parish Magazine*, June 1940.

[25] St Mark's Church Sheffield, Plan of Seating, PR133/13, Sheffield Archives.

[26] Canon Arthur King, writing in *S. Mark's Parish Magazine*, March 1971.

[27] Minutes of St Mark's PCC, 3 April 1940.

CHAPTER 4

DESTRUCTION AND SURVIVAL 1940-60

Tim Moore

'To keep this spirit and tradition alive until such time as we are able to rebuild the Church is the great work that lies before us. The next few years will be a testing time for all of us. If I am to succeed in the great work of reconstruction, I shall need all the backing that you can give me. I am prepared to tackle the job if you will support me.' Canon Gleave, letter to the congregation, 30 December 1940

12 December 1940

At 7.15am on Thursday, 12 December 1940, the last service was held in the old St Mark's. That afternoon British monitoring stations detected X-Gerät radio beams lining up over the north of England. The bombers would follow a principal beam that was intersected by two other beams at precise intervals, pin-pointing the location of the target.

Emil Sperle was a navigator in one of the Junker JU88 bombers, alongside the pilot, Karl, the radio operator Rudi, and Heinz the bombardier and gunner. In Emil's log he wrote of the full moon that night, with clear skies. When their plane reached the English coast they flew in blackout, the instruments read by torch light. They climbed as high as possible to avoid searchlights and flak, donning breathing masks and fur as the temperature dropped to minus 30. When they crossed the final beam, nicknamed Elbe, Emil told Karl to lose height and to heat the bomb bay area. Emil describes the scene below the plane: 'We could see flashes of gunfire on the ground. There below us was Sheffield and it was so bright and clear that I could see the courses of the rivers. There was snow on the mountains to our left as we steered to the right.'[1]

Canon Gleave had gone to the Parkin sisters at the top of Beech Hill Road, apparently taking the church keys with him. Gleave would have been a regular visitor since they were elderly neighbours and important members of the congregation. The church at that time, as a precaution against shrapnel damage, had its windows boarded up.

A yellow alert was issued to Sheffield at 6.15pm, followed by a purple at 6.45, the red alert coming at 7pm, when it was absolutely certain that Sheffield was going to be hit.

Mr and Mrs Temple, St Mark's parishioners for 20 years or so by 1940, were having a rare day together as Mr Temple had a 24-hour pass from the RAF. When the sirens went off at 7.15 they went for shelter in the cellar of their house near the top of Newbould Lane. Writing in the King Edward VII School magazine, a school boy named only as G.H.H. said that no one took much notice when the sirens went off, which would suggest that false alarms happened frequently. Even when the planes were heard overhead, his family stayed in the warm sitting room, not wanting to go down into the damp shelter beside the house. Margaret Braybrook, then 26, was in the family cellar, converted to a shelter, along with all the neighbours. John Carter, another pupil at King Edward's, had fled to the shelter at the side of his house.

As Emil sighted the city, noting the flares intended to mislead the bombers, he called to Heinz to release the bombs. The bomb bay crew counted the bombs out through the hatch, seeing 12 flashes in a row beneath them.

G.H.H. and his mother heard 'a nightmarish whoosh' and dived under the table just as an explosion blew in the windows, shrapnel singing as it hit the walls. When they emerged, his mother found that the strap of her handbag had been sliced by a piece of shrapnel. The Taylors similarly had their windows shattered, by the strike on the Boots shop at the top of Newbould Lane. Under an eerie, light-green sky, earth raining down from nearby explosions, G.H.H. and his mother ran for their shelter, only to find it flooded, so they escaped to the neighbours, just as the sound of drones began to be heard overhead. For John Carter, the bombing was drowned out by the sound of anti-aircraft guns at High Storrs.

An incendiary bomb, or probably several, came through the roof of St Mark's and landed amongst the wooden pews. One fell into the organ, the bellows and pipes a perfect air conduit for building a fierce fire. The boarded windows hid the blaze as it consumed the wooden furniture and roof supports. The Taylors, still sheltering, could smell the wood smoke strongly.

The alarm, when raised, came at a difficult time, since there were many other fires to deal with, including those at Nether Edge Hospital and Neepsend Gas Works, which meant that St Mark's was largely left to burn. Some efforts were made, however. Mr W. Carter Wigg, a part-time auxiliary fireman attached to the Burgoyne Road fire station, had already fought one fire that night before being sent to the church to assist a crew already there. He describes the church as having no roof and the nave being feet deep in 'blazing timber'. There was difficulty finding a mains hydrant since the water pipes had also been hit by a bomb and Carter Wigg ended up on a branch hose trying to fight the fire at the north porch, the doors reduced to charred wood, still attached to the strap hinges. At 9.30, he was relieved from the pump for tea and biscuits at the Nurses Home on Broomfield Road. At 10.30, Carter Wigg's crew were ordered to move on and help elsewhere, leaving the original firemen to fight the blaze. The biscuits he had eaten an hour earlier proved to be his last food for 12 hours.

The attack went in waves, lasting until around 4am. Sheffield was heavily hit, and the west end of the Cathedral was destroyed. A 500 kg bomb fell on the C&A building on Fitzalan Square and another on the Marples Hotel opposite, killing at least 70 in just that one strike. G.H.H and his mother left the shelter when the all-clear was sounded, going to bed in a chilly house with no windows. Emil Sperle and his crewmates warmed themselves with a bottle of Bordeaux wine and hot coffee as they flew back across the channel.

41. The east end of the bombed church, showing the pulpit and reredos.

The next morning, John Carter went to King Edward's school with his father, who taught there, and was apparently relieved that St Mark's had taken the hit and not the school. The church's spire and walls had survived, but the rest was a smouldering wreck. Many refugees from the surrounding areas had been moved into the school to spend the night. John had the job of cleaning the classrooms that morning. Margaret Braybrook came out of the shelter in the morning and saw the other side of the street flattened, with rubble everywhere. She worked at a sewing and knitting shop on Glossop Road, and found that the furniture shop next door had been destroyed. The owner stood in the street, hat on his chest, tears streaming down his face. The other Glossop Road workers tried to help recover what they could from his burnt-out building. G.H.H. was woken by his father, who had driven from Grimesthorpe through the night and the tail end of the Sheffield Blitz. The day after was chaos, with trams left stranded and buildings destroyed. The rebuilding would take far longer than many imagined.

42. Canon Gleave surveys the ruins.

Gleave wrote in a letter to the congregation, dated 30 December:

> There is only one thought in our minds at the moment and that is the calamity that as befallen us in the destruction of our Church. For some months now, ever since the intensive bombing began, we have heard of the destruction of churches, historic buildings, and the homes of the people. And now the blow has fallen upon us and we have been called to share in the sufferings and losses of others.

Rescue and Survival

Only the tower and the walls remained of the once-proud Victorian church. The inside and roof were burnt, the stained glass windows smashed forever. Picking through the remains, it was discovered that the safe in the vestry had survived, preserving the collection plates and the processional cross. The lectern was recovered as well, along with the Great War memorial tablet, which would eventually find its way into the rebuilt church, surviving to the present day in the north-east porch (see Figure 24 on page 26). Scrap metal was salvaged from the site, such was the need of the war effort. And then the church was left alone, fenced off, with warning signs put up. The ruins gradually became overgrown with weeds, small trees sprang up and soon it was home to owls and pigeons. Over the years, despite warnings not to, small children would creep in and play among the blackened walls.

The Wesley Church in Fulwood Road offered to share their building for Sunday services, but the parish already had a large, well-appointed hall, rebuilt only seven years previously (see Figure 37 on page 39). Although it was only a temporary measure, the hall was nevertheless well-suited to its new purpose. William Wilcockson remembered that an alcove between the two fire exits made a 'satisfactory' sanctuary, with an altar on loan from the Revd George Needham of St Anne's Church

43. The bombed church from Broomfield Road, showing how the tower and walls had survived.

on Hoyle Street, Netherthorpe. The recovered lectern was cleaned up by Rowland Williams and used as the pulpit. The Revd Swallow and Mr Williams were congratulated for making the hall 'pleasing in appearance and an atmosphere of sanctuary achieved'.[2] It was noted that there was no provision for kneeling.

There was little change to the services: evening prayer still occurred in the afternoon because of blackout regulations. Funerals and baptisms were held in the hall, but it was never licensed for weddings – which took place at St John's, Ranmoor, with Canon Gleave officiating.

The choir took pride of place up on the stage, directed by Cyril Cantrell. They were initially accompanied by a borrowed piano, but in 1941 an American organ was donated, and then in 1948 the church bought a Compton Electrone organ for £1,600.[3] Despite the slightly make-shift circumstances – the impossibility of an organ voluntary required processional hymns to be used while the choir entered and left – Cantrell maintained a high standard, even putting on the Christmas service of Nine Lessons and Carols.[4]

John Trigg started as a choir boy in 1943, when he was eight years old, despite not living in the parish. He described the method of payment as being a system of coloured tickets. As a new starter he was put on the probationary green ticket, which was only worth a half-penny. After demonstrating his enthusiasm and reliability for about six months, he was promoted to the orange ticket, worth one penny. As he grew older, he went up through different coloured tickets, culminating in the red ticket, worth threepence. Every Christmas, some of the choir would go to the Royal Infirmary to sing carols, led by the 'very demanding' Cyril Cantrell. When his voice broke in 1951, John left the choir and was presented with 'The Marvels and Mysteries of Science' as a prize, having risen to be a soloist in the boys choir.[5]

The hall had less than half the number of seats than the church, which meant drastically reduced collections, leading members of the PCC to call for the choir to be disbanded. This was dismissed, with a resolution to maintain it.

46

The parish hall hosted all the activities accustomed to being held there before the bombing: Scouts, Mothers' Union and Young Wives groups. Fortunately, the Broomspring Lane Mission Hall was also available, and A.E. Cotterill remembered an Easter Garden being built there on a platform by the Sunday school, with sand two inches deep, planted flowers and a sepulchre constructed of a fire guard and branches. A little girl sat in front as Mary and the other children gathered around to sing Easter hymns.

44. Children decorating the Easter Garden at Broomspring Lane Mission Hall during the war.
(Courtesy of Pam Broadhurst)

The Crescent Green, which had been leased to Dr Ernest Finch to produce an income for the church, was used by the Finches for allotments and produced, according to Margaret Wilcockson, 'a lot of food'.

In 1941, the Revd Swallow left to become an RAF chaplain, leaving the parish – and Gleave – without a curate. He saw duty in West Africa and attained the rank equivalent to squadron leader, maintaining a connection with the RAF long after returning to civilian life in 1946.

The '40s brought more departures from the church and PCC. In 1941, Miss F.L. Tozer died, leaving £1,000 to the church Endowment Fund, which brought it up to over £10,000. Mrs Wrightman passed away in 1943, leaving her house, 8 Beech Hill Road, as a clergy house, along with £1,000 for the ground rent. As there was no curate, it was leased for £120 per year to the Royal Infirmary to house nurses. In 1947, V.B. Elliot died, having resigned as one of the PCC joint treasurers only two years previously. Then, in 1948, Mr E.T. Northend resigned after 23 years as secretary of the PCC, and was presented with cutlery and plate for his service.

When St Anne's eventually requested the return of their altar, a new one was designed by the architect George Pace. This altar, along with its frontals, is still used by St Mark's, placed now in the

Lady Chapel of the new church.

Much later, in 1963, Michael Adie wrote that, while the destruction of the church was a great loss, it brought the congregation into a 'closer and more friendly understanding of one another', as opposed to the 'stiffness and formality' that existed before the bombing, when St Mark's had picked up a reputation for being 'rich and supercilious'.[6] The years without a Victorian building put paid to that.

Starting the Rebuilding

In 1945, Gleave turned his attention to going forward with the building of the new church and wanted to get an appeal and a search for an architect underway. Understandably, an informal collection was already taking place for the new church. However, in the same year, the Archdeacon of Sheffield launched an appeal for £750,000 to fund the building and staffing of 10 new churches. The Archdeacon's Church In Action appeal was intended to last for two years but was extended by six months to reach its target, much to the annoyance of the St Mark's PCC, who felt they could not launch their appeal at the same time.

St Mark's raised £4,201 for the Church In Action appeal by 1948, while only raising £860 7s 2d for the restoration of their own church. In addition, in 1948, despite St Mark's lack of a building and falling attendance, the diocesan quota was increased by 20%. Financially, the church was looking at difficult times. Added to that, eight other churches were also hit during the Sheffield Blitz, leaving some parishes, which lacked a parish hall, in a much worse position than St Mark's and needing preferential treatment.

In October 1948, the PCC agreed that the vicar should approach the three 'most outstanding ecclesiastical architects' of the day. They needed an architect not just for the design but also to chase the rebuilding claim with the War Damage Commission (WDC). Gleave sought advice from Dr F.C. Eeles, secretary of the Central Council for the Care of Churches, who had been collecting details of English parish churches to aid restoration after wartime damage from as early as 1939. Major George Pace came to their attention through the Dean of York Minster, Eric Milner-White.

George Pace developed a passion for the gothic as a child from drawing churches with his father. He won the 1937 RIBA Asphitel Prize for the best architectural student in England and was influenced by Charles Rennie Mackintosh, William Morris and Walter Gropius. His designs reflected this mix of the modern and the conservative: the sleek, bare space of the

45. George Pace on scaffolding at Llandaff Cathedral in 1955. Picture from Peter Pace, *The Architecture of George Pace* **(London: Batsford, 1990), p. 2.**

Bauhaus with the decorative folk flourishes of the Arts and Crafts Movement.[7] Pace met Dean Milner-White while working as Supervising Architect to the War Department, Northern Command. The Dean found in Pace a fellow enthusiast for traditional craftsmanship. Pace was made Conservation Architect to Wakefield Diocese in 1948 and in the following year became Surveyor to Sheffield Diocese. He was appointed by the PCC to be the architect of the new church and taken to see the ruins of the old church to discuss what was to be done. Gleave announced he had 'every confidence' in Pace. [8]Michael Adie, Vicar of St Mark's during the rebuilding in the 1960s, described

46. The south-west elevation in Pace's original 1950 design, showing his early ideas for joining the old and the new.

47. The east end in Pace's 1950 design, showing above the altar a great Tree of Jesse to be worked in golden mosaic.

Pace as 'brilliant, delightful and elusive'.[9]

The PCC saw the first plans for the new St Mark's in March 1950. They included a Tree of Jesse mosaic above the altar, 'strong enough to withstand the Sheffield grime'.[10] In April, the Archdeacon gave a talk on church architecture and in May there was a meeting between the PCC, Pace and the Archdeacon. Concerns were raised at the lack of an east window and the position of the choir stalls. By June 1950, the plans had been accepted, but with a few amendments, such as the lavatories and an entrance onto Broomfield Road. The seating capacity was reduced to 450, partly in acknowledgement of falling attendance, but also due to concern over how much compensation would come from the WDC. (For the ground plans of Pace's various designs for St Mark's, see Appendix 5.)

A year later, however, the project was no further ahead, stalled by Pace's illness. A brochure about the rebuilding was printed, explaining the plans of the new building, along with a glowing introduction from the Archdeacon and drawings of the bold new design. However, at a PCC meeting in December 1951, Pace admitted that negotiations had not only stalled, but would have to start again because of the delay.

In 1952, the 63 year-old Gleave had a seizure. Overwork and stress were blamed, and the Revd Graham Neville, then Anglican chaplain of Sheffield University, was recruited to help in 1953. His initial Sunday duties soon exploded into much more.

49

The Parish Action Group

Working on the premise that the new church would be built in two to three years' time, the Revd Neville pointed out at the 1955 PCC AGM that they could either sit around waiting, or do something in preparation. Using as a basis for discussion the 1954 book *The Parish in Action* by Joost de Blank, the Bishop of Stepney, he proposed they set up a group to examine what the laity could do to draw new members to the new church.[11] Stage two, he said, would be practical action leading up to the opening of the new church.

Neville wanted to emphasise that the group would not be a clique with a 'special say' and to reject any suggestion that their work would not be of interest to the rest of the church.[12] They led with the question of who would attend the new church; would it be just the 'faithful few' who had stuck with St Mark's over the previous 15 years? Two principles were agreed: that St Mark's was a parish church and had responsibility for everyone who lived in the parish; and that this active concern must be shared by the members of the congregation as well as the clergy. They planned to visit every household in the parish, drumming up support and interest in the new church. The first groups went door to door at Michaelmas, 1955, then again on 3 October. By the following Easter, they had visited 300 households, signing up 50 of them to the electoral roll.

By August 1956, all of the parish north of Glossop Road and Clarkehouse Road had been visited. There had evidently not been the uptake that had been hoped for and Neville criticised the 'polite goodwill which shows no sign of developing into anything more'.[13] The group did, however, concede that the work had raised the profile of St Mark's.

The Cold War

The nuclear standoff after World War II and political persecution in the USSR occupied Gleave's writing throughout the '50s. He reflected towards the end of the decade that he had spent much of his life either at war or under the threat of war.

When Britain began designing its own nuclear weapon, Gleave considered that the existence of the bomb itself did not make war inevitable, since dictators were afraid of defeat. However, the seriousness of such weapons was not lost on him – a bomb going off in Liverpool, he said, would wipe out all life from the Irish to the North Sea. Man, he said, had the means to destroy the whole human race, and, unfortunately, fear itself was only a frail or temporary deterrent.[14]

The USSR regime, Gleave said, was still Stalinism: enslavement, torture, murder, and a war against God. He utterly distrusted any proposal by the USSR and the Red Army that they would live in peace with Christian people. When, in 1956, the Labour leader, Hugh Gaitskell, and the Shadow Foreign Secretary, Nye Bevan, invited the Soviet leaders, Marshal Bulganin and Nikita Khrushchev, to the UK, Gleave argued that they evidently did not know the history of post-revolution Russia, since in the USSR socialists like Gaitskell and Bevan would be 'no better than vermin'.[15] Gleave despaired of British politicians who would do anything for peace. The Suez Crisis later that year prompted Gleave to describe Gaitskell as: 'stable as a weathercock in a storm'. Similar criticism was levelled at the indecisive Arab states and the United Nations Security Council.

Gleave was, however, able to see a positive side of Communism as a political approach. When the British inflation rate rose above 7%, he said that, had it been Russia, 'the problem would be solved overnight'.[16] He blamed calls for higher wages, arguing that the 'economy is strengthened at the cost of blood, sweat and tears of the people', that political gain should be rejected in favour of the truth, and workers should 'make such sacrifices for our salvation'.

At Gleave's final Remembrance Sunday in 1958, he reflected that war had been a constant presence in his life. He thought that the country had not been prepared in 1914, or to face Hitler. As these wars had shown, he said, appeasement was useless, negotiations with the USSR were a waste of time and the conflict would engulf the whole world: the Russians were, after all, arming themselves while their people starved. The names of all those from the parish who had died during the two world wars were read out in the service. 'Ingratitude,' he said, was 'the most contemptible of human weaknesses.'[17]

Chasing the Money

In 1955, a second set of plans for the new church was submitted to the PCC. The new version was more elegant, with a curved east wall and the worship space footprint in the form of a shield. The chapel had been moved to the north, the flower room away from the vestry, and the organist got an entire balcony to him- or herself, far from the reduced choir of 30. The church was also enlarged, on the basis that more money would be available from the WDC. Members of the Council politely drew Pace's attention to 'the regrettable delay which had occurred since the previous plans were approved'.[18] Nevertheless, the new plans were given the go-ahead and Pace assured them that a quantity surveyor and a consultant engineer would soon be appointed and tenders obtained by October 1956. This was the first time Pace had given them a date.

By September 1955, all the seven companies asked to quote for repairing the tower and spire had

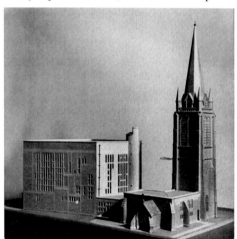

refused due to the risks involved. Pace suggested to the PCC that it was safer and quicker just to wall up the two arches of the tower. This surprised and angered Gleave, who thought that this had already been decided upon. Despite the set-back, Pace was confident that the foundation stone would be laid by the summer of 1956. If it were any later, the PCC knew they would lose generous donors.

As if in a conspiracy against the rebuilding, the winter budget of Chancellor R.A. Butler dealt with the runaway inflation – which had already devalued much of the money raised for the church – by increasing taxes, thus driving up the cost of the build. In addition, there were worrying calls to halt expensive national schemes, such as compensation from the WDC.

48. The north-west elevation in a model of Pace's 1955 design, which eventually proved too large and expensive.

By the start of 1956, Pace reported that an acoustic analysis had been done and he had engaged an engineer for the reinforced concrete sections. Pace was even looking at designs for carpets. The Diocesan Registrar had given approval, but only for the previous set of plans. And then, towards the end of 1956, more delays were announced by Pace, making it impossible to set a date for the laying of a foundation stone. The final drawings – which he had promised a year previously – were to take another six months. And he blamed Sheffield by-laws for 'not allowing the building of stone in a scientific or rational manner', thus forcing him to redesign the formation of the walls.[19] He feared that, because of this, defects would emerge in 150-200 years. The roof structure also needed to be redesigned, since, Pace argued, the construction he proposed had never been used in Britain. He was able to announce that an exhibition of his drawings for the church had been received well, being critically hailed by the *Manchester Guardian* which called it 'the most striking model in the architectural section'.[20] Gleave politely requested copies of the working drawings for the next PCC meeting in November.

In January 1957, Pace told a poorly attended PCC meeting about the modified plans. He now thought the foundation stone could be laid in late summer that year. The Council, in optimistic good faith, said the third week of September would be more convenient. The appeal target for the St Mark's contribution was set at £10,000, with £8,000 for the furnishings. The restoration fund stood then at around £13,000, leaving only £5,000 more to be raised. Another appeal was to be launched after Christmas.

Confusion quickly arose. When Ernest Hayes and Mr Hartley were pushed for financial clarity in February, it was discovered that the estimate for the cost of building had gone up by £5,000, which the congregation would have to raise. The committee naturally decided the figures had become too problematic. It was decided that the plans should be changed to meet the requirements of the WDC, so the appeal target could still not be confirmed. In May, John Heys, Town Clerk and master civil bureaucrat, was given the unenviable task of chasing both Pace and the WDC on behalf of the church.

In June 1957, the process descended into farce, when the meeting set for 18 June between Pace and the PCC to discuss which builder to employ had to be postponed, since the submission date for tenders was not till the 29th. And there was still no word from the WDC. The Parish Action Group had by this time finished its work, covering the whole parish in two years, although several of the most enthusiastic members of the Group had left, frustrated by the continual delays.

By October, with attendance dropping, the PCC considered it unlikely that they would be able to raise a large fund. They requested the WDC to tell them what changes were needed to make the proposed church meet the Commission's definition of 'plain'. Such a building could be paid for by the WDC on a 'cost of works' basis.

Despite all the delays, Gleave stuck by Pace, stating in May 1958 that there was 'no reason to drop him now'.[21] It is evident from correspondence that the cause of the delay was the WDC price calculations, which were based on a 'conceptual church', with buttresses, plinths, window tracery, internal arcades and open timber roofs, i.e. a traditional Victorian church and a cubic footage of only 251,316 ft³. The plans for the new St Mark's, as of 1958, showed a very different, plainer style of building, and far larger, at 449,757 ft³. The disagreement meant only two-thirds of the amount needed was being offered, leaving a shortfall of some £30,000. The more the delays stretched on, the less relevant the initial plans, now 10 years old, became, making further redesign necessary.

On 9 September 1958, the Revd Graham Neville left St Mark's and Sheffield University for the parish of Culworth and Eydon in Northamptonshire, a country parish that would allow him time to write. Despite his 'sincere sympathy' for the building project, it was clear the parish visitations had been wasted.[22]

A few Sheffield students travelled to help decorate Neville's new rectory. And the parting gift raised from St Mark's amounted to £89, which Gleave regretted could not be more. After the induction in Culworth and Eydon, Neville shook hands with all the members of his new congregation. He went on to be Chaplain at Christ Church Training College in Canterbury, then Diocesan Director of Education in Lincolnshire.

Gleave's prospective new curate, Ian Botting, a New Zealander who had rowed and played rugby for Oxford, was set to be appointed on 28 September, but he went back to New Zealand.

As 1959 began, Heys tentatively reported that the WDC were re-calculating their figures. By April, it was announced that, having put aside their inadequate conceptual model, the WDC were prepared to pay £71,165 for the building, and £7,809 for the stained glass. The costs for the demolition of walls and repairs to the spire were still to be chased. The amount was readily accepted by the PCC, who must have felt that, after so many years, they had finally prevailed.

At this landmark moment, Pace was paid his fee of £1,420. During negotiations for the next stage, an impasse was reached when Gleave, the PCC and even the bishop wanted the building work to be conducted under a fixed price contract. Pace, however, was determined that such a scheme would never work. The PCC and the rebuilding committee had a special meeting to decide whether to retain Pace, knowing that letting him go would mean not only finding a new architect, but also having new plans drawn up. They decided to keep him on.[23]

In June, after years of holding the parish and the rebuilding project together through failing health and old age, Gleave announced his retirement, effective from October. At 70, he had been waiting for a significant milestone before leaving, and the announcement from the WDC must have seemed like the end of the struggle.

In his farewell letter of October 1959, Gleave spoke of his arrival in April 1931, and of the 1930s when there was a period of increased prosperity as the allies rearmed for World War II using Sheffield steel. He remembered the loss of life and property during the war, but also the revolution in social conditions and habits. He said he saw the previous 14 years as a painful process of recovery, during which the large houses around the old church had become schools, offices and flats. His old friends, his way of life, he said, now belonged to another generation, another world. The Revd Michael Adie, writing in 1963, said, 'That there are still so many of [the] pre-war generation of worshippers with us now is itself a visible seal of his effective ministry maintained for so many years, even during ill health.'[24]

A special farewell service was held, at which Gleave was presented with a radio, a reading lamp and a cheque for £487. His wife received a handbag from the Mothers' Union and tokens for roses from the Young Wives group, both organisations that Dorothy Gleave had helped run over the years. They moved out of the vicarage, but only up the hill to Taptonville Road, staying close to the parish and parish life.

Canon Rodgers, recently retired from Tankersley and now living in the parish, was requested to take Sunday services, which he did with 'the utmost cheerfulness and efficiency, to the great advantage of the parish'.[25]

In July 1959, John Heys recommended that the current plans for the church be completely abandoned and Pace be instructed to come up with a simpler building that would match the money coming from the WDC. Despite the PCC being told that this change of plan would cost them an additional £1,838, it was approved. An east window was requested – a matter raised early on and yet never included. These new plans, when completed the following year, would eventually become the new St Mark's.

But then disaster struck. The Diocese Reorganisation Committee (DRC) withdrew permission to rebuild and told the PCC to purchase the Glossop Road Baptist Church, now the University Drama Studio on the corner of Glossop Road and Clarkson Street. The DRC also had a plan to abandon St

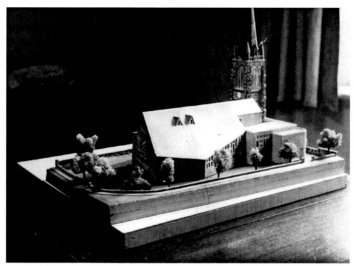

49. Model of Pace's final design for St Mark's, produced in 1959-60.

Mark's and divide the parish among its neighbours. This must have been an especially bitter pill to swallow, since not a penny for the rebuilding was coming from the diocese. The diocese favoured switching the WDC money to new housing estates, which were much more in need of new churches than the west of Sheffield. It also claimed the St Mark's congregation was not big enough to justify the rebuilding and, if they did go ahead, questioned whether they would be able to maintain the church and vicar. After so many years of delay and frustration, this was especially poignant, since it was the delays that had been a substantial cause of the dwindling attendance.

The Bishop of Sheffield, Leslie Hunter, was invited to two special meetings held on 24 November, one with just the PCC, led by William Wilcockson and Ernest Hayes, the other with the congregation. The DRC's Baptist church proposal was discussed and it was explained to the bishop

that the Baptist church was too far away from the centre of activities in Broomhill, and the interior decoration offended the aesthetic sense of some, particularly with the enormous baptistery in the sanctuary. The bishop left, saying he had been 'impressed with the strength of feeling' among the congregation.[26]

In January 1960, the church wardens, Wilcockson and Hayes, were able to announce that the diocese had given the go-ahead for the rebuilding. After a last-minute lurch back from the precipice, the project was finally nearing completion and, having spent two decades worshiping in the church hall, the faithful remnant would at last see their hard work fulfilled.

50. Bishop Leslie Hunter, a 'strategist of the spirit', but taciturn and not easy to know.

Notes

[1] Emil Sperle, in *Memories of the Sheffield Blitz in Heeley and Thereabouts* (Sheffield: The Heeley History Workshop, 2010), p. 50.

[2] Minutes of St Mark's PCC, 21 April 1941.

[3] Minutes of St Mark's PCC, 21 April 1941 and 14 October 1948.

[4] William Wilcockson, writing in *S. Mark's Parish Magazine*, April 1971.

[5] Email from John Trigg, dated 5 December 2012.

[6] *S. Mark's Parish Magazine*, August 1963.

[7] Peter Pace, *The Architecture of George Pace* (London: Batsford, 1990), p. 14; See also 'George Pace' in Wikipedia.

[8] Minutes of St Mark's PCC, 15 November 1948.

[9] Interview with Michael Adie, 29 April 2012.

[10] Pace, *Architecture of George Pace*, p. 181.

[11] Joost de Blank, Bishop of Stepney, *The Church in Action* (London: A R Mowbray & Co Limited, 1954).

[12] *S. Mark's Parish Magazine*, August 1955.

[13] *S. Mark's Parish Magazine*, August 1956.

[14] *S. Mark's Parish Magazine*, May 1955.

[15] *S. Mark's Parish Magazine*, May 1956.

[16] *S. Mark's Parish Magazine*, October 1957.

[17] *S. Mark's Parish Magazine*, November 1958.

[18] Minutes of St Mark's PCC, 18 October 1955.

[19] *S. Mark's Parish Magazine*, November 1956.

[20] Pace, *Architecture of George Pace*, p. 182.

[21] *S. Mark's Parish Magazine*, May 1958.

[22] *S. Mark's Parish Magazine*, August 1958.

[23] *S. Mark's Parish Magazine*, June 1959.

[24] *S. Mark's Parish Magazine*, August 1963.

[25] William Wilcockson, writing in *S. Mark's Parish Magazine*, April 1971.

[26] *S. Mark's Parish Magazine*, December 1959.

Chapter 5

THE NEW ST MARK'S 1960-9

David Price

a radiant addition to Sheffield architecture – Sheffield Telegraph, 27 September 1963.

My greatest joy has been the free and family atmosphere of the Christian community, which in Broomhill increasingly means the Anglican/Methodist community. … There is both in our worship and our activities a family atmosphere – and I don't mean just noisy children stampeding around (though that happens at times) but there is an openness of mind, a readiness to discuss problems from first principles, a framework of community which enables us to disagree vigorously and yet remain in the same family. Most of all, I suppose it is the assumption that we are all together trying to work out what God means us to do in the world today, that we all have to contribute and to learn, that I have most enjoyed and from which I have most benefited. (Michael Adie's farewell message, December 1969)[1]

In the 1960s, the modern St Mark's Church took shape – not just the building, but also a new ethos of openness of mind and community spirit.

The 1960s marked an extraordinary turning-point in English church history. Adrian Hastings writes of 'a very sharp shift away from organised religion of any kind – a shift quite unprecedented in speed and spread'. The number of men entering the Anglican priesthood fell from 636 in 1963 to 393 in 1971. Similarly, confirmations and church membership declined. Michael Ramsey, Archbishop of Canterbury, commented: 'It may be the will of God that our Church should have its heart broken.'[2] The reasons have been much debated, with some blaming the furore surrounding *Honest to God* by the Bishop of Woolwich. It is more likely that traditional belief and behaviour were profoundly disturbed by the trends towards individualism and the 'permissive society' that marked this decade.

Unlike many churches, St Mark's expanded greatly in the 1960s, from on average 30 communicants each Sunday in 1961 to 170 in 1965 – a level that continued thereafter with various ups and downs.[3] The new building of course played its part, but there were also great strengths in the young Vicar and the congregation.

Leading the Church

Michael Adie's arrival as the new Vicar of St Mark's in August 1960 marked a dramatic generational shift in leadership. Canon Gleave had eventually retired in 1959 at the age of 70. By contrast, Adie, the son of an agnostic Essex farmer and a Methodist mother, was only 30. Adie read theology at Oxford and trained for the ministry at Westcott House. He was a curate in the Sunderland shipyards (St Luke Pallion) and then resident chaplain to Archbishop Fisher at Lambeth Palace. He knew all the leading personalities in the Church of England and brought many of them to St Mark's. Leslie Hunter, Bishop of Sheffield, wanted someone to minister to the Teacher Training College in Collegiate Crescent and Clarkehouse Road and encouraged Adie to apply.

Adie was a formidable young man, intellectual (even 'cerebral'), modern in his thinking, energetic, determined and not easily daunted. This is illustrated in the part he had played as Fisher's Chaplain in engineering his master's resignation. Adie knew that the bishops thought that Fisher talked too much and was domineering. Adie talked with Rosamond, Fisher's wife, who encouraged him to speak directly with the Archbishop. So Adie had the invidious task of informing Fisher that the bishops wished him to retire. Fisher listened and then remarked: 'This is very odd, that you, still in your twenties, should be leaning on my mantelpiece telling me, the Archbishop, sitting here that I have to go.' Nonetheless, Fisher took the advice and remained a kind of father figure for Adie.[4]

As Archbishop's Chaplain, Adie had fallen for Fisher's secretary, Anne Roynon. Fisher encouraged Adie by telling him to borrow Rosamond Fisher's car and drive down to seek the blessing of Anne's parents, and the two married. With great grace and social skill, Anne was a vicar's wife of the old school, ceaselessly entertaining people and building up links in the local community. Before services, she would stand at the church door welcoming people. Adie reckoned her contribution was invaluable. Three of their four children were born at St Mark's. Lord Fisher of Lambeth came to St Mark's for christenings. Previously, archbishops of York had only come to St Mark's for the consecration of the church in 1871 by Archbishop Thomson, the institution of Bishop Quirk in 1905 by Archbishop Maclagan and possibly a visit by Archbishop Lang.

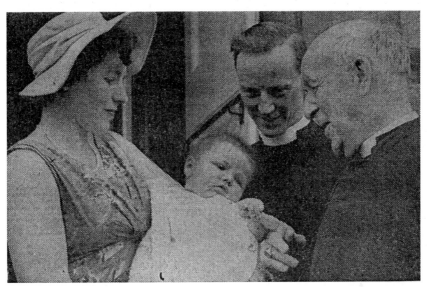

51. Lord Fisher of Lambeth, former Archbishop of Canterbury, at the baptism of Andrew Adie, with Ann and Michael Adie. June 1961 (photograph courtesy of *Sheffield Telegraph*).

Adie's administrative skills ideally suited him to the urgent task of getting the new church built. He was also a man of faith and prayer, to be found at 7am every morning preparing for 7.30 Holy Communion.

He was assisted by a succession of able curates, who generally led on youth work – Ted Longman (later Vicar of St Thomas, Brightside), David Ellington (described as 'highly popular and charismatic'[5]; he was later Priest in Charge at Altrincham, Cheshire) and Andrew Butcher (later Vicar of Holy Trinity, Louth, then an RAF Chaplain).

The spirit of dedication among these clergy and their wives was remarkable, as illustrated by a story told by the Revd John Bowker at the service to mark the 20th anniversary of the consecration of the new St Mark's in 1983. In the 1960s, Bowker had been curate at St Augustine's, Brocco Bank. He recalled:

> At that time I used to go for long periods into borstals as if under sentence and the idea of that was to make some sort of contact and friendship with people there by living the exact conditions of their life. And I well remember arranging with Ted Longman, one of your curates … and his wife (Rose) to take in a young lad, Alan, when he was released from Borstal in order to give him a home. He had no parents, no home of his own. And for a month or two it all worked very well until Ted and his wife went on holiday. When they came back, Alan had completely stripped their home: curtains, chairs – he'd even sawn through some of the lead pipes leading to the basins. Well, you can imagine my feelings

when I heard about this. I remember walking up the hill to see them, wondering what on earth I could possibly say. I rang the doorbell and she opened the door, and, before I could say anything, she said 'Thank you.' And I said, 'What do you mean?' She said: 'Well we're very glad that you gave us the chance to help. We knew when we took Alan in that it would probably go wrong. But if there isn't the chance of it going wrong, he wouldn't have needed help in the first place.' And then she added, 'If you meet anyone else in Borstal who needs a home, please let us know.' Well, among all the things I have forgotten about those Sheffield days, that I do remember. I thought it was such an unbelievable response. And that extraordinary generosity, the memory of that generosity, still plays a part in my life and helps to make me what I am.[6]

Introducing Change

Adie had inherited a congregation that was set in its ways and he pondered how to effect change. He learned much from his first Christmas. Shortly before the 11am Christmas Service, he realised that the service was liable to over-run and told the organist to omit the anthem. The organist and choir went on strike and the organist resigned. But when Adie apologised to the PCC for this incident, one PCC member told him that it was 'the best thing he had done'.

Adie respected the 'old guard', who had 'borne the heat and burden of the day' at the parish hall, but concluded that their dream of re-creating the old St Mark's of the 1930s would not work. It would not build the congregation for George Pace's new church, which would be large, open, welcoming and modern. Nor would it reflect the growing Anglican movement towards Parish Communion as the principal Sunday service.

Adie decided to pursue his own progressive agenda and to encourage those in the congregation who were sympathetic. He introduced parish meetings (borrowed from Alan Ecclestone, famous Vicar of Darnall). He transformed the parish magazine, changing its cover design from old-fashioned fussiness to modern symbolism.

More importantly, Adie introduced Parish Communion and weekly Compline. He realised that this meant having in effect two congregations, since a group led by William Wilcockson, Vicar's

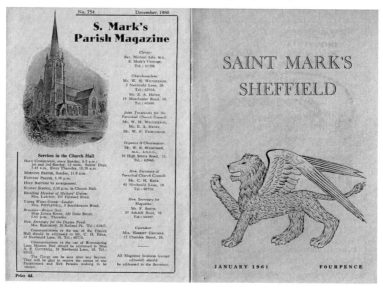

52. Parish Magazine covers for December 1960 and January 1961, illustrating the change of style introduced by Adie.

Warden from 1951 to 1964, and his wife Marjorie, insisted on retaining Mattins. There were other conflicts with the Wilcocksons over stewardship, relations with the Methodists and the Mothers' Union. Adie admired Marjorie's social contribution but upset her by ending separate Eucharists for the Mothers' Union, which he saw as divisive. Disconcertingly, the Wilcocksons would complain to others rather than to Adie direct, forcing him to ask them about these rumoured disagreements. The fact that Canon Gleave lived in Broomhill until 1965 was uncomfortable, even if Gleave did little more than take funerals when any of the older generation died. Fortunately, the division in the congregation was not absolute. The people's warden, Ernest Hayes, built bridges between the two groups.

Gradually, a new generation emerged and took responsibility. We can only mention a few of the members here:

53. Ernest Hayes, Church Warden from 1953 to 1966 and a valuable bridge builder in the congregation (*Mark's Messenger*, April 1989). **Drawn by Pamela Mann.**

- Ann Lewin, who arrived in 1963, a secondary school teacher of English and religious studies, later PCC Secretary;
- David and Pam McClean. David was a young academic lawyer, who represented St Mark's on the Diocesan Synod, later becoming a Professor and Chair of the House of Laity of General Synod (See Figure 69 on page 74)
- Roy and Doreen Godden. In 1965 Roy, a young accountant, became Church Treasurer, serving until 1996 (Deputy Treasurer until 2006). From 1968 to 1974 he was Church Warden as well. His wife, Doreen, contributed enormously to the pastoral and social life of the church and led the Sunday School in the 1970s.
- Robin Saunders, a young research engineer, who joined St Mark's in 1965 and in 1969 married Eve, a music teacher.
- The Revd Michael and Fleur Bayley, who arrived in 1967. Michael was working for his PhD in Social Studies and became a spare time non-stipendiary minister – the beginning of a long involvement.
- The Revd John and Janet Earwaker, who joined St Mark's in 1969. John was a young lecturer at the City College of Education (see Figure 79 on page 90) and Janet a music teacher.

Some of these are still members of St Mark's. They shared with Adie a commitment to change in the Church of England and were inclusive and ecumenical in approach. Most had academic links.

Adie wanted to streamline the cumbersome St Mark's committee system. There was a PCC of 26 members (from 1962 onwards elected annually, rather than for three-year periods)[7] and some 10 other committees. In 1964, he persuaded the Annual Meeting to reduce the PCC to 18 members, but in 1965 it was only by exercising his casting vote that he prevented William Wilcockson's attempt to *increase* the PCC to 32 members. At this time, the congregation was not so widely dispersed as it later became. For example, in 1968 only two out of nine lay officers of the church lived outside the parish. Finally, Adie got it established that Church Wardens would serve for

54. Roy and Doreen Godden.

55. The Revd Michael Bayley.

terms of only four years, whereas William Wilcockson had served for 13 years.

Theology

Adie was a 'liberal catholic'. His 'liberalism' owed much to academics such as Leonard Hodgson, Christopher Evans and Dennis Nineham, and to his experience as curate in the shipyards of Sunderland, which taught him that Biblical language needed interpreting in the common language and ideas of modern society – a view shared by the Industrial Mission in Sheffield. Adie accepted John Robinson's case in *Honest to God* for restating the tradition afresh, but felt that Robinson went too far in denying existing beliefs without clarifying what should be believed. Adie's 'catholicism' again was moderate. He disliked the 'trivia of churchmanship' but valued catholic expressions of worship as aids to prayer and awe before God and went on retreat at Mirfield. His wish to preserve the sacrament in the aumbry in the Lady Chapel caused conflict with Archdeacon Hayman Johnson. Adie was ecumenical and wanted Christians of different traditions, both within the Church of England and, like the Methodists, beyond it, to come together.

The 1960s marked a change in theology at St Mark's. Under Gleave and his predecessors, St Mark's had shared Sheffield's traditional evangelical Protestantism but henceforth it claimed to be in the 'liberal critical tradition' of Anglicanism.

Building the New Church

Adie's independence of mind was illustrated in his attitude to the rebuilding project. In February 1961, he asked Bishop Hunter whether it was right to rebuild at all, as there were already nine churches within a mile of St Mark's. Hunter advised him that the war damage money was there and there were no new factors to justify a rethink, thus saving Adie from a major confrontation with his flock. Later, Adie justified the rebuilding as creating a Christian centre for an area of university buildings, hospitals and schools as well as a residential population of 6,000.

During 1960-61, the plans for the church were finalised by George Pace, the Building Committee, still chaired by John Heys, Town Clerk of Sheffield, and the PCC. (John Heys died shortly before the consecration of the new church.) The Lady Chapel was doubled in size. An Upper Room was planned, with access via stairs from the porch rather than from inside the church (an idea of Bishop Hunter). At Adie's suggestion, the font would be moveable.

Adie worked hard to make the new church happen. His parishioners later commented: 'He has rallied the Committees, chased the architect, the contractor and the sub-contractors, organised the services and checked detail and still more detail with efficiency, accuracy and good humour.'[8]

In August 1961, the PCC accepted Bradbury's tender as main contractor for £80,992, to be provided by the War Damages Commission. On 4 November 1961, Dr Whittaker, Vice Chancellor of Sheffield University, laid the foundation stone. By early 1962, the old building apart from the tower and spire was demolished and work began on the foundations of the new building. Harry Stammers' design for the East window, which was to cost £3,500, was approved. From St Clement's, Newhall, in Attercliffe, St Mark's purchased pews in seasoned Canary wood. The church clock was restored to working order. The church purchased 540 hassocks and 500 copies of *Hymns Ancient and*

Modern Revised. In May 1963, agreement was reached to place a Yorkshire Electricity Board sub-station in the south-east corner of the churchyard.

The project was financially challenging. The WDC did not pay for the furnishings of the church, estimated to cost £19,000. Some of this was found from generous gifts from individuals, but the balance depended on congregational giving. Moreover, it was estimated that the annual running costs of the new church might be £5,500. A Stewardship Committee, led by Lt Col George Field, launched a Stewardship Campaign in 1962 with the paid help of the Diocesan Giving Adviser. This brought in promises of £3,313 a year. There was still some £4,500 to be found for furnishings and an organ from income over the next three years. However, the church had substantial inherited assets, such as the sport's field on Coldwell Lane, which it sold to Crosspool Open Space Committee for £8,445 in 1961.[9]

56. The Stewardship Committee 1962-63. Left to right: William Bird, Mr Blacow, Alan Armstrong, Mr Hartley, Ray Holehouse, Lt Col George Field, Peter Vickers, Ernest Hayes, and the Revd Michael Adie.

Moving into the New Church

On the evening of Thursday, 26 September 1963, a fanfare of four trumpets and a tympanum greeted the Rt Revd John Taylor, the Bishop of Sheffield, as he entered the new church for the consecration. He praised the building as joining 'in one harmonious and ingenious whole something left of the old and something quite new in design'.[10] Somehow, 550 people crammed into the church. Acute appendicitis prevented Lord Fisher of Lambeth from attending. But among those present were the University Vice Chancellor, the Capital Burgess, the heads of local schools and figures from the past including Canon Gleave, the Revd E. Mannering (Vicar 1921-31) and the Revd J. Haythornthwaite (Curate 1903-5). The Archbishop of York, the Dean of Windsor and other church dignitaries also came to other services in this period.

The press noted that this was apparently England's most expensive post-war parish church.[11] Judith Scott, Secretary of the Church of England Council for the Care of Churches, said that the 'quality of the design and workmanship sing their own veritable Benedicite'. But she also said: 'There

57. An early picture of the south-western view of the new church, bringing out the blend of old and new.

are unlikely to be many new Anglican churches ... built to such a standard in the future and some may have doubts as to whether, if we had the money, we could ever again spend it all on one church with an easy conscience'.[12]

Adie urged his congregation 'to avoid becoming absorbed in stained glass, new organs and refurbished boilers, lest we forget people in New Guinea. More organs in England may mean fewer priests in South America.'[13] But he also agreed with Pace's view that 'a church is an act of worship by its very existence'. For Adie, 'The new building symbolised our efforts to break new ground liturgically, theologically and socially.'[14]

At Consecration, the building was complete except for the west window, the Lady Chapel windows and the organ. John Piper's west window, a depiction of the Holy Spirit, was dedicated by the Bishop of Sheffield on 8 December 1963. After much debate, Gillian Rees-Thomas's quiet abstract windows for the Lady Chapel were installed in 1968. (see Figure 98 on page 115)

On 11 October 1963, the temporary electric organ then in use caught fire. Fortunately, Adie and Peter Vickers were in the church and called the Fire Brigade, which quickly came and put out the fire. The building was undamaged. Early in 1965, the Foster and Andrews organ provided by Cousans (Lincoln) Ltd at a cost of £7,655 was installed, on a specification by Dr W.L. Sumner of Nottingham, principal consultant on organs to the Royal Schools of Music. Three hundred people came to hear the first organ recital by Anthea Morton. It was soon recognised as one of the finest organs in Sheffield.

A beautiful church needed beautiful surroundings. Throughout the 1960s, much effort, involving 100 volunteers, went into producing a pleasant vista of the church from Glossop Road, as recommended by an architect, Marshall Jenkins. The workforce was led by Peter Vickers, chartered mechanical engineer and 'a tireless organiser of projects'. The north wall of the Crescent Garden was lowered and the iron railings on the south side of the church removed. The bank in the Crescent Garden was formed by spreading 70 tons of ash on the rubble from the wall and covering that with 60 tons of top soil. The slope up to the church was sown with grass seed, a heather bed was created,

58. A working party energetically building up the bank on the south side of the church (photograph courtesy of *Sheffield Star*).

three small walls were built, one incorporating a gargoyle, known as 'Lady Marks', from the old church. In September 1964, a bed of roses was established on the bank to form a Garden of Remembrance. On one occasion, the workforce was rewarded with a barrel of beer, though several valuable pints were lost when the Vicar's three-year-old son switched on the tap and could not turn it off. Three other familiar features of St Mark's date from this period – the flood-lighting of the east window, the flight of steps from the vicarage to the West door and various asphalt paths round the church.[15]

The Church Hall on Ashgate Road was retained for church groups and the community. It was called the 'Parish Hall', with the Church's Upper Room known as the 'Church Room'. The latter name failed to stick and it remains the 'Upper Room'.

Worship

When Adie arrived, Sunday Services at the Church Hall in Ashgate Road were Holy Communion at 8am (and also at 12 noon twice a month), Morning Prayer at 11am and Evening Prayer at 6.30pm. The only weekday service was 10.30am Holy Communion on Thursdays. Adie changed this pattern. He introduced daily Communion at 7.30am. Then at Advent 1961, he introduced Parish

Communion at 9.15am (later 9.30am) on Sundays. He let Mattins continue at 11am throughout his incumbency, although choirboys became reluctant to attend both services.

St Mark's was adventurous in its worship, introducing a new liturgy, known as the Green Book, at Sunday Communion in 1963. Much to Adie's surprise, Bishop Taylor gave his approval, saying: 'If some us are not prepared to go to the Tower in the interests of modernisation, we shall never make progress.' In 1967, Series 2, recently authorised for 'experimental use', was introduced after discussions and a rehearsal.

59. Refreshments for the working party. Adie is on the far left. Peter Vickers, 'tireless organiser of projects', is drawing beer from the barrel. Mary Richardson is at the table serving refreshments. Ted Longman, Curate, is standing at the rear to the left of the window. In front of him are Victor Gibson and his wife Jackie (photograph courtesy of *Sheffield Star*).

In 1967-8, there were tensions at PCC over whether to introduce Eucharistic vestments designed by Pace, in place of surplice and stole. William Wilcockson thought that this 'Catholic propensity' might put off the Methodists. Adie argued that vestments had 'no doctrinal significance' and eventually secured a majority for their introduction.

With the move to the new building, St Mark's retained its traditional choir of men and boys, led by Bob Johnson ARCO, who became organist and choirmaster in 1962 and would serve until 1988. His day job concerned national and international standards for steel. A choir member of the time recalls Bob's 'extremely high standards'.[16] The choir had long commanded great loyalty from its members. For example, Arthur Millhouse had served as an alto since 1909. In 1968, it was agreed to include

60: Worship in the new church 1963-4. Ted Longman is celebrating and Michael Adie is on the left.

women in the choir, whereupon Millhouse retired. Robes were worn at Evensong but not at the 9.30 Eucharist, at which the choir led the congregation in settings by Williamson and Appleford.

Ecumenical Relations

Ecumenism was a major preoccupation at St Mark's in this period, as it was throughout the Christian churches. At first, St Mark's had two ecumenical partners – Wesley Methodist Church [17] on Fulwood Road and Broompark Congregational Church on Newbould Lane (now part of Sheffield High School). The three churches joined together in services, visiting, and collecting for Inter-Church Aid, but Adie felt that 'this does not get us very far'.[18] In 1968, the Congregationalist congregations of Cemetery Road, Endcliffe and Broompark resolved to unite at Endcliffe, well outside the parish, leaving Wesley Methodist as St Mark's sole ecumenical partner. Adie worked closely with Wesley's Minister, John Farley.[19] Lent Groups began to be run on an ecumenical basis.

Supporting national moves for union between the Church of England and the Methodist Church, the two churches held valuable joint meetings. In 1964, it was agreed that the Anglicans should attend an Evening Communion at Wesley – an unusual step at the time. Adie consulted the Bishop, who feared that it might be divisive if some from St Mark's took Communion while others abstained.[20] The PCC eventually agreed that 'the actual partaking of communion was left to members' personal judgement'.[21] The PCC was divided about ecumenism: one future Church Warden, John Johnson, felt that ecumenism sacrificed principles to the fashion of the day for a very small gain.[22]

Adie was frustrated by the Church of England's growing negativity about the proposed union with the Methodists. Ann Lewin reported misgivings at Deanery level. David McClean wrote, 'It isn't a very Anglican quality, but, please, cannot someone produce a bit of enthusiasm?'[23]

In 1969, the Church Assembly of the Church of England failed to provide the necessary majorities for the unity scheme to go ahead. Adie, by then about to leave St Mark's, proposed to the PCC a joint resolution by St Mark's and Wesley in favour of increasing unity between the two churches, including reciprocal arrangements for Communion. Leslie Fillmore described it as 'a controversial paper to introduce shortly before the Vicar's departure' and the matter was 'adjourned'.[24]

Children and Young People

Outstanding among those working with children was Mabel Green, Head Teacher of Western Road Infant School from 1941 to 1969, who led the Sunday School for many years. In February 1965, the *Broomhill Magazine* commented: 'Sixty or seventy children on an average Sunday may not be the pre-war size of a Sunday School but it shows a vigorous church life.' A former pupil describes Mabel as 'quite formidable … an absolute stickler for getting things right … a tireless and devoted worker for the church'.[25] She was against talking down to children. In 1965, Adie wrote about her Passion play involving 33 children: 'The effect was almost startling. Children doing a Passion play have an emotional effect on adults beyond imagination.'[26] In 1967, she wrote another Passion play about Mother Maria Skobtsova, who volunteered to take someone else's place in the gas chamber.

In 1962, Anne Adie and Jean Farley, wife of the Methodist Minister, founded the Under Fives Group, a play group on Wednesday mornings, in the Church Hall (later at Wesley). In November 1964, the Young Lions group was formed – 10-13-year-olds who met not only during the 9.30 Service on Sunday but also on Friday evenings for 30 minutes' Christian instruction and 30 minutes' 'boisterous games'. In August, St Mark's and Wesley Chapel organised a 'non-stop variety week of activities' for 80 local school children in 1964 and 120 in 1965. Activities included clay modelling, visits to caves, the fire station, printing works and museums, tennis and indoor games.

The Crisis over Club 62 and the Sale of the Parish Hall

61. Mabel Green and other ladies in later years at the Broomhill Festival. Right to left: Mabel Green, Mary Littleton and Monica Smith. The lady on the left has not been identified.

The most problematic youth venture was Club 62, founded in 1962 by Jim Sharp, son of the Broompark Congregational Minister. By 1965, it had a paid youth leader, catered for the age range 14 to 21, and met regularly in the Parish Hall. Its popularity was such that a limit of 70 young people was imposed.[27] Activities included pop music, five-a-side football and discussion groups.

Most of those attending Club 62 had no link with the church. Their erratic behaviour worried the PCC. In 1967, the paid leader needed support by some members of the congregation because of recent trouble with one or two members. In September 1968, the PCC refused to allow football in gym shoes on the Crescent, generating a debate about what the Crescent Gardens were for and whether to retain them. The local authority was not interested in taking them over. Other ideas were to put a hostel or Parish Hall there or rent the space as a car park to the Hallamshire Hospital. But in the end, the PCC made no change.[28]

In January 1969, Ernest Hayes advised the PCC that the Parish Hall was costing around £300 a year and suggested selling it. Andrew Butcher for the Youth Club Management Committee argued that this would damage Club 62 – without indoor football the Club would fall apart. The PCC favoured selling it, provided this would not adversely affect youth work. Butcher's Committee reviewed their strategy and by May had changed their minds. They now proposed to close down Club 62, having lost faith in their ability to manage it: 'In recent years ... we have merely gathered young people off the streets and not known what to do with them. ... The club has from time to time got completely out of hand.' It was thought best to concentrate on the Young Lions on Friday nights in the Upper Room.[29] As a result, after 95 years, the Parish Hall was sold to the City Council and became a library store and later a block of student flats (see Figure 37).

62. Broomhill holiday week (photograph courtesy of Andrew Braybrook, born 1951, who is in the centre).

Reaching Out

St Mark's was an outward looking church. In July 1964, the parish magazine declared, 'Broomhill is still a place in which people of reforming zeal and civic service live and work.'[30] The same could be said of St Mark's. The parish boundaries changed in 1961 as a result of a diocesan review. St Mark's gained from St Thomas, Crookes, some streets immediately north of Broomhill shopping centre, while it lost to St Silas the Broomspring-Brunswick area of Broomhall, including the Mission Hall, which it now loaned to St Silas.[31] (See figure 71 on page.76)

Broomhill was changing. Institutions of all kinds – industry, schools, colleges, universities and hospitals – were taking over more of the parish. The university, endlessly expanding, threatened to remove 400 houses between Crookesmoor Road, Marlborough Road and Harcourt Road. St Mark's supported residents' movements in that area and Broomhall Park. An architect warned: 'Broomhill has become a short term community. By 1966 approximately 1500 students will commute daily during 30 weeks of the year between Endcliffe and Western Bank.'[32]

Many university staff, particularly medical staff, attended St Mark's. Adie learned much from Lawton Tonge, Professor of Psychiatry, and later recalled him saying: 'People go to a psychiatrist expecting to be understood; they go to a priest fearing they will be judged. That is why our waiting rooms are full and your vestries are empty.'[33]

63. Left to right– Professor Lawton Tonge, Ann Tonge, Anne Adie and Michael Adie at Windsor. The occasion and date are unknown. William Lawton Tonge, Professor of Psychiatry at Sheffield University, died in 1976. Lawton Tonge House, a centre for mental health, was founded in his memory in Nether Edge. Ann remained a member of St Mark's congregation until her death in 2011 (photograph courtesy of Charlotte Tonge).

Adie found St Mark's relations with students problematical. Bishop Hunter envisaged Adie ministering to the Teacher Training College and Jack Churchill at St George's ministering to Sheffield University, with co-ordination by a committee. But, as this Committee seemed ineffective, Adie sought to build up St Mark's parish life in the hope that students would join.

St Mark's people contributed to many social initiatives, including Norman House for ex-prisoners in Upperthorpe (1963), St Agatha's Hostel for unmarried mothers (1968), the new

Abbeyfield Society house for elderly people in Marlborough Road (1969) and various schemes for visiting old people and invalids living alone, which developed in 1965 into the Sheffield Churches Committee (later Council) for Community Care (SCCCC).

There was much interest in visiting within the parish. In 1969, it was found that 44% of homes had some religious affiliation, 13% were Anglicans attending a particular church and 12% Anglicans with no church connection.[34]

Sheffield's economy also was changing. Sheffield's steel and cutlery industries, which had seemed so formidable, faced new challenges from foreign rivals. Roger Sawtell (see below) warned of increasing redundancies.

There was growing awareness of local poverty. A Sheffield group of Child Poverty Action Group was formed in 1968. Andrew Butcher, Roy Godden and others stayed up for a couple of nights to seek out the homeless and found so many that a hostel for vagrants was established at Bethlehem House, Hanover Way, which St Mark's supported till 1994.[35]

The Vicar's income had long been enhanced by rental from a glebe property, 8 Beech Hill Road, for years an outpost of Birkdale School. When it became vacant in 1965, the PCC eventually did a swap with the NHS for 442 Glossop Road, which became self-contained flats.[36]

In January 1961, the PCC decided that 10% of gross income should be given to the church overseas, following a resolution from the Church Assembly of the Church of England.[37] Following representations from the Overseas Committee, this rose to 13% by 1965 with a further 7½% going to home donations.[38]

Relations with the Bishop

Adie had enjoyed excellent relations with Bishop Hunter, but in 1962 Hunter retired to be replaced by John Taylor, former Principal of Wycliffe College, Oxford. (see Figure 65 on page 72) Unfortunately, Taylor suffered a stroke which prevented him from taking up his duties until 1963. Taylor's illness may have affected his subsequent behaviour, which Adie felt was 'conservative, authoritarian and unimaginative'.[39]

Conflict erupted at Sheffield Industrial Mission, when Michael Jackson, Ted Wickham's successor as Senior Chaplain, sacked two theologically radical chaplains. The ensuing furore reached the national press. Taylor sided very strongly with Jackson. St Mark's had long supported the Industrial Mission; one of its members, Roger Sawtell of Spear and Jackson, was Secretary to the Senior Managers' Group of the Mission. Adie criticised a Working Party, set up by Taylor to resolve the dispute, as weak on ecumenism and overlooking the Mission's role in 'sharing God's work in the world'.[40] Adie's theology was broader than Taylor's individualistic evangelical Protestantism.

Adie's difficulties with Taylor, however, arose mainly from Taylor's authoritarian management style. Adie served on various key diocesan committees, but felt that Taylor did not respect their role in decision making. In July 1967, Taylor expected the Board of Finance to approve the diocesan budget before it had been drawn up. Adie refused. Taylor accused Adie of not trusting him, but Adie argued that committees had to work co-operatively, not by diktat.

At diocesan conference in 1968, Adie challenged an attempt by the Provost, Ivan Neill, an ally of the Bishop, to present resolutions as coming from the Diocesan Committee on Mission and Unity, when they did not. Neill backed off, but Taylor subsequently moved Adie off this committee. Taylor also vetoed articles and letters that Adie wrote for diocesan publications and Archdeacon Hayman Johnson rebuked Adie for causing problems with the Bishop. Adie felt he was in danger of being thought of as Leader of the Opposition in the diocese, which was not good for him or the diocese.[41]

Adie's Departure

Adie felt that he had to move and accepted an invitation from Kenneth Riches, Bishop of Lincoln, to become Rector of a new team ministry based in Louth. He could not reveal the main reason for his departure. In July 1969, he announced that he would leave at the end of the year, writing, 'I have been here in Broomhill now for nine years and the pace of the life of the church here seems to be losing some of its impetus: so it seemed right that both Broomhill and I should have a change.'[42] Later he told the congregation:

> Strange for these days, it means a reduction in salary and 'status': I shall resign as rural dean, proctor in Convocation and a member of the Church Assembly of the Church of England. Abdicating responsibilities? In one sense, yes and with a good conscience. It is debatable whether the decisions which really affect the life of the church are always made in Lambeth, Millbank or Westminster. I think they are made in the parishes where people actually live and work.[43]

Adie became Archdeacon of Lincoln in 1977 and Bishop of Guildford in 1983. Tragically, on Christmas Day 1978, Anne Adie suffered tubercular meningitis, which left her impaired mentally and physically.

At St Mark's, Adie had released much talent, insight and energy. The foundations for the new St Mark's were laid.

Notes

[1] *Broomhill Magazine*, December 1969.
[2] Adrian Hastings, *A History of English Christianity 1920-2000* (London: SCM Press, 2001), pp. 535-6 and 550.
[3] Michael Paton, *Broomhill Magazine*, June 1978.
[4] Letter from Michael Adie to the author. See also William Purcell, *Fisher of Lambeth* (London, 1969(, p. 290.
[5] Recollection of Andrew Braybrook.
[6] Sermon by the Revd John Bowker on 2 October 1983.
[7] Minutes of Annual Meeting. 3 April 1961.
[8] Letter from 'Parishioners' in *Broomhill Magazine*, November 1963.
[9] Minutes of St Mark's PCC, 27 October 1960 and 2 March 1961.
[10] *Sheffield Telegraph*, 27 September 1963.
[11] *British Weekly*, 26 September 1963.
[12] *Anglican World*. No 2, Easter Whitsun 1964. pp 42-5.
[13] *Broomhill Magazine*, November 1963, referring to a report from the Toronto Anglican Congress, *Mutual Responsibility and Interdependence in the Body of Christ*.
[14] Letter from Adie to the author.
[15] Minutes of St Mark's PCC, 25 January 1963. *Broomhill Magazine*, November 1964, February 1968 and November 1970.
[16] Recollection of Andrew Braybrook.
[17] Wesley Church building was demolished in 1982 and Broomhill Methodist Church, now renamed the Beacon at Broomhill, was opened in February 1998.
18 *Broomhill Magazine*, January 1963.
[19] *Broomhill Magazine*, March 1968.
[20] *Broomhill Magazine*, June 1964.
[21] Minutes of St Mark's PCC, 19 June 1964.
[22] *Broomhill Magazine*, October 1968.
[23] *Broomhill Magazine*, October 1967.
[24] Minutes of St Mark's PCC, 10 October 1969.
[25] Recollection of Andrew Braybrook.
[26] *Broomhill Magazine*, June 1965.

[27] *Broomhill Magazine*, January 1965.

[28] Minutes of St Mark's PCC, 17 February 1967, 4 March 1968, 12 September and 21 October 1968.

[29] Minutes of St Mark's PCC, 29 January and 2 May 1969.

[30] *Broomhill Magazine*, July 1964.

[31] Minutes of St Mark's PCC, 27 June 1960 and 25 March 1961.

[32] J. Marshall Jenkins ARIBA on the Future of Broomhill. *Broomhill Magazine*, May 1963.

[33] *Broomhill Magazine*, 1 November 1981.

[34] Minutes of St Mark's PCC, 26 March 1969.

[35] *Broomhill Magazine*, September 1970.

[36] Minutes of St Mark's PCC, 14 May 1965, 22 March 1968 and 11 December 1968. In the mid 1970s, 442 Glossop Road passed to the diocese as a glebe property. It was later sold by the diocese to Sheffield University who used it until 2007, when it was again sold, with St Mark's receiving a windfall payment of £9,650, as a share of the fee for lifting a restrictive covenant.

[37] Minutes of St Mark's PCC, 17 January 1961.

[38] Information from Roy Godden.

[39] Letter from Adie to the author.

[40] *Broomhill Magazine*, August 1967.

[41] Letter and emails from Adie to the author.

[42] *Broomhill Magazine*, July 1969.

[43] *Broomhill Magazine*, December 1969.

CHAPTER 6

THE SEVENTIES AND MOST OF THE EIGHTIES 1970-87

David Price

'St Mark's is a loving accepting community but one does not realise this until one has got into it. Like the church building itself, the image we present outwardly as a congregation is rather formidable. The solution is not obvious, we need to increase our openness to one another and to outsiders. It does not appear that this increased awareness can be planned nor should we become self-conscious about it.' Report of a PCC discussion in 1973.[1]

Adie left his successors a new model of an Anglican church – strong in its spirituality, lively, experimental, liberal – all in a dazzling contemporary architectural setting. The next two decades would test this new model.

Nationally, these were turbulent years of high inflation, industrial relations conflict and increasing political polarisation. Sheffield lost much of its traditional industry and its left-wing Council became a centre of resistance to the Thatcher Government. In 1984, South Yorkshire was a battle ground of the Miners' Strike. Church people worried about high unemployment.

St Mark's faced big changes close at hand. In 1978, the closure of St George's Church brought a larger parish, new members and new links with the Anglican chaplaincy to the University. Also in 1978-9, the Royal Hallamshire Hospital opened on St Mark's doorstep.

Leadership

The Vicars in this period – Michael Paton from 1970 to 1978 and John Giles from 1978 to 1987 – shared much of Adie's vision. Paton's father was a Presbyterian Minister and Secretary to the International Missionary Council, but Paton's mother became Anglican and then Roman Catholic. Before ordination, Paton had been in the Indian Armoured Corps, Oxford University and the Diplomatic Service. After Lincoln Theological College, he was Vicar of St Chad's, Woodseats, and then Senior Chaplain to the United Sheffield Hospitals. He was married to Margaret, a former nurse, and by 1970 they had five children, who found St Mark's people friendly and welcoming.

Paton had strong sympathy with people facing serious illness or even death. After coming to St Mark's, he was Chaplain to Weston Park Radio-Therapy Hospital, which he visited at least twice a week. He was a founder member of the Telephone Samaritans.

Paton had a relaxed leadership style and was content to let a thousand flowers bloom. His congregation included six university professors, one of whom told him: 'You don't need to match academic ability, but we want you to say what you think.'[2] Paton found life at St Mark's satisfying but extremely busy, particularly after he became Rural Dean of Hallam Deanery. In 1978, he accepted Bishop Gordon Fallows' invitation to become Archdeacon of Sheffield.

Bishop Fallows invited John Giles, his former student at Ripon Hall Theological College at Oxford, to apply for the vacancy at St Mark's and Giles got the job. Fallows came to St Mark's to institute John Giles – an enormous effort for him as he was already terminally

64. The Revd Michael Paton, Vicar from 1970 to 1978 and then Archdeacon of Sheffield.

65. Michael Paton's institution as Vicar in February 1970.
Left to right: Bishop John Taylor, the Ven. Hayman Johnson,
Archdeacon of Sheffield, and Michael Paton (photograph
courtesy of *Sheffield Telegraph*).

ill with cancer.

John Giles was aged 43, a Cambridge rowing blue, sailor and son of a famous naval architect. He had set up the Anglican Chaplaincy at the new University of East Anglia and served as Rector of Kidbrooke in Greenwich. He was married to Jill, a teacher of English literature, who resisted any attempt to typecast her as vicar's wife (not that anyone at St Mark's ever tried) but still exercised a wide ministry of friendship, practical care and hospitality.

Giles found St Mark's very different from Kidbrooke. In April 1980, he told the Annual Meeting that:

His first year in the parish had shown the difficulties caused by the diverse viewpoints of members of the congregation, though they were also its strength. He felt that development in two directions was needed: first, a deeper sense of waiting upon God and second more work on outreach to the parish. [3]

Giles' emphasis on outreach was reflected in his becoming a part-time Industrial Chaplain with Sheffield Industrial Mission at Viner's historic cutlery works until they closed down. He was subsequently Chaplain at Harris-Miller and Staybright (Forgemasters).

St Mark's curates in this period were Andrew Butcher up to 1970, Philip McFadyen from 1971 to 1974 (a qualified art teacher, who with the young people created in 1973 the splendid mosaic of the Flaming Lion, still in the church vestibule: see Figure 97 on page 114), and finally David Gay from 1975 to 1978. After this, St Mark's had no curate until 1991, increasing the pressure on the incumbent. In 1987, Giles commented that St Mark's did not qualify for a curate 'as the size of the church was considerably reduced from former times'. [4] However, university chaplains became attached to St Mark's (see below).

66. The Revd John Giles, Vicar from 1978 to 1987, and the green altar frontal donated in 1982 by Michael Blagden, Verger from 1952 to 1988, in memory of Michael's wife Maureen (photograph courtesy of *Sheffield Telegraph*).

67. Jill Giles.

Other clergy also assisted at St Mark's. Michael Bayley continued his spare-time role. He was increasingly busy, not only as a lecturer in Social Administration but also as a member of the Social Policy Committee of the Church of England's Board of Social Responsibility, for which he masterminded a report in 1986, *Not Just for the Poor: Christian Perspectives on the Welfare State*.

In 1981, the Revd John Earwaker became Chaplain to Sheffield Polytechnic and, like Michael Bayley, frequently preached and led services at St Mark's. In 1976, the Polytechnic had taken over the teachers' training college located within St Mark's Parish and was renamed Sheffield City Polytechnic.

Theology

Paton was a 'Prayer Book Catholic and a moderate liberal'. He did not see St Mark's as particularly radical or intellectual, just educated. He saw Christianity as a search for truth in life, which involved making mistakes. His tolerant attitude helped to foster an unusual spontaneity and audacity about St Mark's approach to theology. In 1971, John Earwaker wrote in the parish magazine about 'the image of Christ as a dancing Lord', pointing out that, as the early church became respectable, merriment was frowned upon.[5] Michael Bayley led a group entitled 'That I can't believe'. Paton's friend, David Jenkins, later the *bête noire* of traditionalist Anglicans, began his association with St Mark's by leading a weekend seminar in 1976. (A later picture of David Jenkins at St Mark's is at Figure 92).

John Giles' approach combined Anglican 'catholic' insights with respect for biblical scholarship and theology, tempered in the secular culture of the University of East Anglia (characterised by Malcolm Bradbury's *History Man*). Giles favoured openness and tolerance and helped to found an Open Church Group in Sheffield, becoming its Secretary. He sustained the links with David Jenkins and was dismayed later on by calls for Jenkins, now the controversial Bishop of Durham, to be disciplined. Giles told the congregation that, if this occurred, he would resign.

In this period, women were beginning to play a more prominent role at St Mark's. In 1974, the Annual Meeting voted by 26 to 16 in favour of allowing women to be 'sidesmen'. In 1980, Giles secured the Bishop's agreement that three women should administer the chalice at the Eucharist. In 1984, St Mark's appointed its first female church warden, Margaret Lyons. At General Synod level, David McClean was chairing committees involved in the long haul towards the ordination of women.

Deanery, Diocese and Beyond

Sheffield Diocese became more settled after the retirement of Bishop John Taylor in 1971, even if, as David McClean warned, 'by English standards (it was) numerically and financially very weak'.[6] Taylor's successor, Gordon Fallows, was liberal in theology and emollient in leadership style. Paton was close to Fallows as he suffered the tragic loss of a daughter and a son and then fell ill with cancer himself and died. Fallows' widow, Edna, remained a member of St Mark's congregation for many years. Fallows was succeeded in 1979 by David Lunn, a Geordie Anglo-Catholic.

St Mark's made a big contribution to the Diocese, with seven people from St Mark's serving on Diocesan Synod in 1973. One of these, David McClean, moved right to the heart of Church of England decision-making, being from 1979 Vice Chair of the House of Laity of the General Synod, then Chair from 1985 to 1995, and from 1977 to 1985 a member of the Crown Appointments Commission, involved in the appointment of bishops. From 1980 to 1984, he was one of St Mark's Church Wardens.

Worship

Paton inherited from Adie the problem of Sunday Mattins, which continued until 1975 when the PCC at last agreed to abandon it. The PCC had many intense debates about liturgy. Paton argued that 'accepting things we don't like … can be a corrective to spiritual selfishness'.[7] In 1973, the introduction of Series III liturgies at the Eucharist was agreed following its ratification by General Synod. The Gloria came early in the service – its pre-Reformation position – and people stood for the Thanksgiving.

In 1980, the PCC approved the experimental use of Rite A for the Parish Communion Service. 200 copies of the red Alternative Service Book were bought. In 1982, Giles commented that Rite A 'has not had an altogether friendly reception', with 'criticisms of its lack of poetry, resonance, style and so on'. He defended it as having more of the great doctrines of Christianity than the 1662 service.[8] In 1985, some felt that this service was 'too long, too busy, too wordy, too rushed'. Rosalind Rogerson produced a booklet of Taizé chants to be sung instead of the opening hymn, but there were 'very strong views for and against'. In 1987, David McClean, who helped to authorise liturgies at General Synod, asked why St Mark's adopted a style of service different from most other churches.[9]

68. Bishop Gordon Fallows and his wife Edna.

In 1972, the British Steel Corporation, now in the historic Mount building nearby, gave St Mark's a processional cross. After considerable argument at PCC, this was used to lead the procession at Parish Communion. In 1979, the son of Canon Gleave presented a Paschal candle stick in memory of his father.

A roving Commissioner from the Royal Schools of Music described the choir as 'of considerable ability', despite 'the awkward placing of the choir stalls and the difficult acoustics'.[10] Various settings were used at the Eucharist, including Salisbury, Dankworth, Williamson, Hurford and Wiltshire. But Bob Johnson, organist and choirmaster, felt that this service offered little scope for the choir and that those who did not attend Evensong did not realise the quality of the choir.

The Closure of St George's

The closure of St George's, Portobello, in January 1978 greatly affected St Mark's. St George's had similar churchmanship to St Mark's, was very active on social and international issues and had links with the Chaplaincy for Higher Education. Nearly all its congregation lived outside the parish. In 1977, they decided on closure because of the depleted parish population and the shift in the centre of gravity of the University, and because they could not afford to maintain the Grade 2 listed building. St Mark's PCC agreed to take on most of St George's parish when Bishop Fallows promised some money for extra staff. St Mark's acquired 'all that part lying West of Upper Hanover Street and North and West of Glossop Road'.[11]

69. David McClean, Professor of Law at the University of Sheffield, Church Warden, 1980-4, and Chair of the House of Laity of General Synod, 1985-95. He master-minded the legislation for the ordination of women.

70. St George's Church, Portobello, which closed in 1978, causing the enlargement of St Mark's parish. Many of the congregation joined St Mark's (photograph from Odom's *Memorials of Sheffield*).

In 1981, owing to the closure of St Nathaniel's, Crookesmoor, St Mark's additionally acquired Harcourt Road, a recreation ground and one side of Crookesmoor Road (see Figure 71 on page 76).

The closure of St George's brought an influx of energetic lay people who soon played a major role in St Mark's, such as George and Margaret Atherton, Roy and Beryl Barry, Arthur and Winifred Golding, Linda Kirk, Margaret Lyons, Gordon Powell, Trevor Adams, Florence Wood and Ron and Mary Ellis.[12] They mostly arrived at St Mark's on 15 January 1978.

Relations with the University

With the closure of St George's, St Mark's became involved with the University Chaplaincy and more students came to the church. In June 1978, the Revd Peter Wills became assistant priest at St Mark's and associate Anglican Chaplain to the University, alongside Father Edmund Wheat of the Society of the Sacred Mission. When Wheat left in 1980, Peter Wills became full-time Chaplain and in May 1980 organised at St Mark's the University's Centenary Thanksgiving Service. Soon after this, the Revd Chris Irvine became joint Chaplain alongside Peter Wills.[13]

Initially, the student presence was greatest at Evensong. In 1980/81, the chaplains led five University Evensongs, followed by student discussions in the Upper Room on subjects such as 'The Contemporary Novel'. The 9.30am Parish Communion unfortunately clashed with breakfast at the halls of residence. The chaplains called for a later service and eventually, in 1984, the time was changed to 9.45am.

St Mark's reached out to students, with special services to welcome them in early October and 'hospitality Sundays' when families in the congregation invited students to Sunday lunch. Some students helped with the Sunday school and other youth work. The PCC co-opted a student representative.

In 1984, Chris Irvine was replaced by the Revd Jonathan Clatworthy, who later became General Secretary of the Modern Churchpeople's Union (now Modern Church).

Even in Chris Irvine's time, students were being drawn away elsewhere, notably to St Thomas, Crookes. Under Robert Warren's leadership, this church had been radically remodelled, re-opened in 1980 and was increasingly charismatic. Its lure increased when the Nine O'Clock Service (NOS) began in 1986. St Mark's and the Chaplaincy found it hard to compete with the rock bands and stunning visual effects of the NOS. But Giles worried about the apparently cultish behaviour of NOS's charismatic leader, Chris Brain.

Outreach

The opening of the Royal Hallamshire Hospital in 1978-9 was a challenge to St Mark's. At the request of the hospital chaplain, a St Mark's team escorted patients from their wards to the hospital chapel for the 11.00am services. St Mark's musicians led a monthly session of hymn singing for patients. There was also concern about mental health and St Mark's gave lasting support to the aftercare of psychiatric patients at a new Sue Ryder Home, Wootton House, in Beech Hill Road.

There was great interest in pastoral care in the parish. In 1970, 'street wardens' distributed the

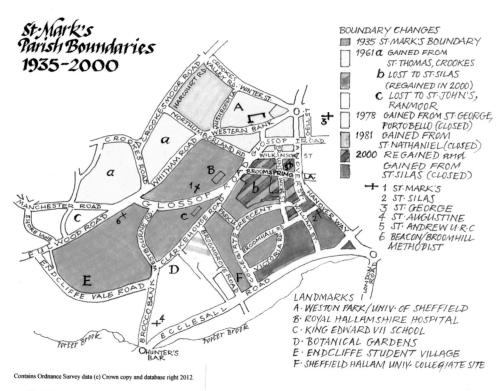

St·Mark's
Parish Boundaries
1935-2000

BOUNDARY CHANGES

- ▨ 1935 ST·MARK'S BOUNDARY
- ☐ 1961 *a* GAINED FROM
  ST·THOMAS, CROOKES
  - *b* LOST TO ST·SILAS
    (REGAINED IN 2000)
  - *c* LOST TO ST·JOHN'S,
    RANMOOR
- ☐ 1978 GAINED FROM ST·GEORGE,
  PORTOBELLO (CLOSED)
- ☐ 1981 GAINED FROM
  ST·NATHANIEL (CLOSED)
- ▨ 2000 REGAINED and
  GAINED FROM
  ST·SILAS (CLOSED)

- ✝ 1 ST·MARK'S
- 2 ST·SILAS
- 3 ST·GEORGE
- 4 ST·AUGUSTINE
- 5 ST·ANDREW U·R·C
- 6 BEACON/BROOMHILL
  METHODIST

LANDMARKS I
A · WESTON PARK/UNIV· OF SHEFFIELD
B · ROYAL HALLAMSHIRE HOSPITAL
C · KING EDWARD VII SCHOOL
D · BOTANICAL GARDENS
E · ENDCLIFFE STUDENT VILLAGE
F · SHEFFIELD HALLAM UNIV· COLLEGIATE SITE

Contains Ordnance Survey data (c) Crown copy and database right 2012.

71. Map showing changes in St Mark's parish boundaries in the twentieth century (David Bradley).

Broomhill Magazine and, later, cards at Christmas and Easter. From 1978, Ronald Ellis, a geographer from St George's, joined the Pastoral Care Committee. With restless energy, he reorganised the areas for pastoral visiting and introduced training. Between Paton's departure and Giles' arrival, Ellis and the Pastoral Care Committee organised an information system under which 76 members of the congregation manned the phone. This lapsed when the new Vicar arrived. In 1984, following a pilot by the Ellises in Harcourt Road, 29 members of the congregation[14] visited 487 dwellings. In 1987, Ellis came up with a scheme to tighten further the system of Pastoral Group 'leaders', but this was rejected by most PCC members as too 'organised'. Ellis resigned from the Pastoral Care Committee as 'his heart had been entirely bound up with the proposals'.[15]

The Miners' Strike of 1984 disturbed many people at St Mark's. In October 1984, Giles persuaded the PCC to authorise a collection at the Parish Communion for the Dearne Valley Churches Hardship Fund to help 'victims of the miners' strike';[16] £165 was collected, a significant sum in those days.

The congregation was also disturbed by the massive increase in unemployment, which stimulated the Anglican *Faith in the City* Report of 1985. John Giles set up a small group from the City Council, the Manpower Services Commission and the Industrial Mission to explore options, but progress was difficult. Giles favoured links with the less affluent parish of St Silas, Broomhall, which was in Ecclesall Deanery. In 1985-6, the Diocese questioned St Silas' future, but proposed links with St Mary's Bramall Lane or St Barnabas, Highfields, rather than with St Mark's.[17]

Since the 1970s, St Mark's was also in the vanguard on recycling. Tony Crook collected 12.48 tonnes of paper and cardboard from the congregation.

Nor were overseas links neglected. Roy Barry, a former national Chair of the World Development Movement, became Chair of St Mark's Overseas Committee in June 1978 and put great energy into this work. In 1984, he became City Organiser for Christian Aid. He helped to

72. Roy Barry reading part of a short service in Broomhill shopping centre on Palm Sunday 1987 with John Giles to his right.

ensure that St Mark's made a big contribution to the May Day Trek and the collections for Christian Aid Week and kept up its level of international donations at 13% of given income.

The Building

Heartfelt tributes were paid when George Pace died in 1975, but certain practical limitations of his building were increasingly recognised:

- Inadequate storage facilities. Eventually a storeroom was created behind the west window.[18]

- Provision for tea and coffee after Parish Communion. The original assumption was that people would go to the Upper Room, but many never made their way upstairs. From 1983 onwards, the Choir Vestry was used, apart from a brief reversion to the Upper Room in 1985-6.[19]

- The acoustics of the church were poor, perhaps because the original sound-absorbent panels had been painted in a redecoration. It was agreed in 1981 to install a speech amplification system.[20]

- Disabled access. The International Year of Disabled People triggered a review in 1981. Additional hand rails were installed and for a time the 'funeral door' (or 'east door') was opened before Parish Communion to help disabled people get into the church. However, a lift for access to the Upper Room seemed too expensive.[21]

- Car parking. The Royal Hallamshire Hospital and the expanding University caused increased 'unauthorised' car parking. In the church car park, a chain was installed in 1973. But problems in the Crescent were more intractable.[22]

Resources

High inflation caused anxiety about money. Several business people in the congregation lost their jobs. In 1982, Roy Godden, the Church Treasurer, told the PCC: 'St Mark's congregation had proved extremely capable of talking about things but not doing them: the time (has) come for some radical rethinking of our direction as a congregation.' Apparently 'a stunned silence followed Mr Godden's impassioned remarks …'[23] Enthusiasm for stewardship campaigns fluctuated. In 1985, the Stewardship Campaign was launched with a buffet supper at Halifax Hall. 'Group ralliers' then visited eight households each. The campaign also invited offers to volunteer and 'suggestions' for improvement (such as calls for an all-age choir, a curate, reviving the parish magazine, children's services, greatly increased overseas giving). This campaign successfully brought in £8,651 gross, which, among other things, made it possible to set up the Vicar's Discretionary Fund to provide confidential help to people in special need.[24]

St Mark's had substantial assets, including the proceeds from the sale of the Ashgate Road Parish Hall in 1971 and of the Mission Hall in Broomspring Lane, Broomhall, which the Council bought for £6,500 in 1979.[25] The Council made it a community centre, which it still is today. (See Figure 18 on page 23). In 1980, David McClean led an Assets Committee to consider what to do with the money, but, apart from repair work carried out on the church and the organ, the money was kept in reserves. The next incumbent would be astonished by the Church's assets.

The Broomhill Festival

Broomhill was becoming more community-minded. In 1973, the Broomhill Action and

73: Broomhill Festival Garden Party on St Mark's Green in June 1985.

Neighbourhood Group (BANG) was formed to strengthen residents' voices in planning decisions. Then in 1975, the idea of a Broomhill Festival emerged in the Department of Architecture at the University. There were concerts, exhibitions in the Library and the Mappin Gallery, an open air art exhibition and the Broomhill Show. It was 'a marvellous opportunity to start drawing the community together. Community spirit is not dead but rather "out of fashion"'.[26] The Festival became an annual event every June. Members of St Mark's such as Ann Lewin, Robin Saunders, Fleur Bayley, Doreen Godden and Pauline Miller helped organise the Festival and drew in members of the congregation. Arguably, the Festival became over-dependent on St Mark's. There was a Festival Service at St Mark's to which the Lord Mayor was invited. The Festival helped local charities, but its prime aim was to draw the community together.

Children and Young People

The sale of the Parish Hall meant that some weekday youth activities took place at the excellent new YMCA premises in Broomhall Road and some in the Upper Room. In 1972 and 1973, St Mark's joined up with the YMCA to run 'holiday adventure weeks' for 8-13-year-olds in the summer holiday, with as many as 180 children participating in 1972. In 1973, the children were encouraged to discuss the meaning of Christian life during lunch-time breaks. It was discovered that they 'found it extremely difficult and puzzling to talk about God for they really had little idea who He is'.[27] On Friday nights, the Upper Room was the venue for a youth club, whose leaders were proud that over four years only two lights had been broken. Half of those attending came from church families and half not. Meanwhile, during the Parish Communion on Sundays, a new pattern was established in 1973 whereby the various junior church groups (including for a time John Hillman's teenage group) met during the earlier part of the service and came into church shortly before Communion.

Many adults worked hard for young people and those efforts increased in the 1980s.[28] In 1980, Rosalind Rogerson reintroduced the 3rd Sheffield (St Mark's) Girl Guide Company after a break of 24 years. Judith Brown led the St Mark's Brownies. By the mid-1980s, there were five groups for children

74. The third Sheffield (St Mark's) Girl Guide Company, revived in 1980 by Rosalind Rogerson (top row 2nd from right).

and young people meeting during the service – crèche, Little Fish, Sunday School and Junior and Senior Lions.[29] John Giles and John Hillman led two parties of young people on memorable weekends in Edale.

Ecumenical Relationships

The high hopes of the 1960s for a national reconciliation between the Methodists and the Church of England were finally dashed in 1972, when the unity scheme failed to get a large enough majority in the new General Synod. St Mark's PCC reassured Broomhill Methodists of their wish to work closely together.

The Wesley Methodist Church building in Fulwood Road needed rebuilding, but for more than 20 years every rebuilding plan fell through. In the early 1970s, some in both churches favoured making Broomhill an 'area of ecumenical experiment'. At St Mark's, David McClean argued that buildings should not keep Christians apart. At Wesley, the Revd Bob Figures and Donald Smith proposed in 1973 that St Mark's Church should be a shared worship centre (with mainly separate services for the two congregations), while Wesley would be replaced by a jointly run 'Christian centre' offering education, facilities for groups and bedrooms for students and a resident Christian community. This scheme was accepted by St Mark's and would have cost £15,000, but early in 1974 Wesley abandoned it when a developer offered to rebuild at zero cost. In the event, however, this scheme, like others, failed to get off the ground.[30]

In 1982, the Wesley building was finally demolished and the Broomhill Methodists began to worship at Tapton Congregational Church. In 1984, it was agreed that the Wesley congregation would join St Mark's for a united service once a month. Then Wesley's situation changed again as Wesley amalgamated with Carver Street Methodist Church. Eventually, this enabled the Methodists to rebuild with their own money, but the new Methodist Church in Broomhill would not open until 1998.[31]

St Andrew's United Reformed Church became closer to St Mark's in this period. In January 1982, St Andrew's joined with St Mark's and Wesley for the Methodist Annual Covenant Service. St Andrew's also joined with St Mark's and Broomhill Methodists in Lent Groups.

In September 1977, the Chinese Christian Fellowship started to use the Upper Room regularly.

Drama at St Mark's

St Mark's tradition of drama and musical plays dates from this time. In 1979, Mary Almond produced a Nativity Play on Christmas Eve, an event that has continued to this day. In 1986, Giles, a Britten enthusiast, and others staged Britten's *Noyes Fludde* as part of the Broomhill Festival. As Britten envisaged, it was truly a community production, with Shelagh Marston, Mary Grover and Eve Saunders training 60 children from the congregation and local schools to play animals and birds. Alan Brown mobilised the University Music Department. An ark was constructed in the sanctuary. This was the first of a series of major productions over several decades.

Holding Together a New Kind of Church

St Mark's had evolved into a partly 'gathered church' attracting people from a wide area, as well as from within the parish. The congregation was becoming more diverse and more demanding, as described by Michael Paton in 1975:

> The laity take the initiative quite a lot, many of them are highly skilled in widely differing fields, they expect their views to be listened to and are more likely to argue about the sermon than to say how wonderful it was. [32]

St Mark's was not an easy church to lead. Decades later, Michael Paton described the congregation as 'intelligent, kindly and wanting to be true Christians. Result: a happy Vicar. Rewarding, very.' [33] But a close observer recalls him saying more than once in the 1970s: 'Things could all fall apart at any time.' [34]

75. Noah's ark in the sanctuary for the production of Britten's *Noyes Fludde* in 1986 (photograph: Eve Saunders).

One way to bring the congregation closer together was through parish weekends, like that led by David Jenkins in 1976. There were also many small groups. In 1983, around 100 people attended Lent groups, some of which became permanent. Three groups merged to become the Contemplative Prayer Group (often known just as 'The Group'), which still exists today, extending beyond St Mark's. At this time, it consisted of young professionals facing problems of work and bringing up children; they met regularly in people's houses. About 30 people would attend an annual weekend gathering with a pattern of silence, prayer, talks and discussion, including sharing personal problems. New people were invited to join. Ideas bubbled up for improvements at St Mark's.

The problem of how to integrate newcomers into a large congregation preoccupied Paton and the PCC (see the opening quotation of this Chapter). Some practical steps were taken, which helped. In 1977, it was decided to 'welcome' people as they came into church for the Parish Communion and in 1978 a weekly notice sheet was introduced.

Paton felt that further growth was held back by the difficulties of caring for those who were already there. In 1978, he wrote

> There is much careful evidence to show that congregations all over the country tend to stick around 150 (with variations, of course, depending on many other factors) whatever the size of the parish. … in St Mark's … a graph of communicants from 1960 to 1977 shows a rise to about 170 in 1965 and thereafter with various ups and downs a level line at around the same figure, 170. Surely we can't be content with this self-limiting structure? … Our present pattern of friendship and care doesn't adequately fit our needs … there is still a kind of caring deficit. The Vicar alone cannot make it up. … The PCC and many others are working at this…'[35]

Paton's departure prevented him from seeing this through. His successor, John Giles, also worried about lack of cohesiveness in the congregation. He felt that the problem was that different groups were pulling in different directions – practical people from business, the Contemplative Prayer Group and other groups, medical people, academics, musicians, chaplains, students, advocates of

76. St Mark's congregation in 1987, assembled on the grassy slope at the south-west corner of the church (photograph: Michael Miller).

political or social action, deliverers of children's activities, social events, etc. As there were thought to be too many committees, David McClean led a review in 1979, which eliminated a few but added a Study Committee. Among the sources of tension for church leadership at this time was finance, affected by Sheffield's de-industrialisation and widespread redundancies. Roy Godden, Church Treasurer for 31 years, recalls 1978-84 as the most difficult period he experienced. In 1981, Giles reminded the PCC that 'all the activities of the church were the joint responsibility of myself and the PCC'.[36]

In 1982, Bishop Lunn carried out a Visitation of St Mark's. His subsequent Bishop's Charge picked up issues such as welding the congregation together and mission.[37] In 1983, Giles told the congregation that 'although the idea of mission did not generally seem to appeal to St Mark's congregation, this must be the focus of the coming year'.[38] On Sunday, 10 June 1984, some 150 people from St Mark's joined 15,000 other church people at Doncaster Racecourse for a gathering to mark the beginning of the Diocesan Year of Mission. St Mark's pledged to visit every house in the parish.

In 1985, there was a Billy Graham Crusade in Sheffield. Opinions were divided at St Mark's, but Giles eventually got the PCC to support the Crusade 'at least to some extent' – a classic St Mark's qualified reaction.[39] A committee was formed to work with the Crusade and the PCC donated £100. St Mark's booked 320 seats at the rallies, and 293 of them were occupied. 122 members of the congregation attended at least one rally and five 'nurture groups' were set up to help those from the parish who 'came forward' during the rallies.

In 1985, Giles referred to 'a certain lack of corporate involvement in St Mark's as a united church body. There was a danger of creating too many sub-groups and he felt that more intermingling of different activities should be encouraged.'[40] In 1986, he said: 'We should spend less time lobbying for our particular cause. ... We should be united together in worship and prayer.'[41] Early in 1987, he organised a PCC training event: 'Where is unity? How does worship unite us?'[42] Looking back, Giles believes that these efforts did achieve greater unity.[43]

Giles' Departure

At the Annual Meeting in April 1987, Giles referred to 'the pressures on our lives and the need for strong faith to know God's will for the world. He prayed that His mercy would overrule our inadequacies.' He concluded that 'beauty, peace and worship are to be found in St Mark's Church'.[44]

In June 1987, John Giles departed with Jill to Baltimore for a four-week swap with an Episcopalian Minister. Just before his departure, Giles unexpectedly received two job offers, one of which was an invitation from Frank Curtis, Provost of Sheffield Cathedral, to become a Residentiary Canon at the Cathedral. The timing was difficult, but Giles was attracted by the opportunity of a new city-wide ministry, seeing different sides of Sheffield's life. So in September, he announced that he was leaving St Mark's for the Cathedral. He told the PCC that some of the difficulties he had faced could be alleviated by the employment of a caretaker and ideally a curate, though St Mark's size did not at that time warrant the latter.[45]

Paton and Giles both brought considerable gifts and commitment to St Mark's and worked fruitfully with their talented and varied congregation. Many classic features of St Mark's originated in these two decades, including involvement in the Broomhill Festival, the tradition of drama and musical plays, and the links with the University Chaplaincy and the Royal Hallamshire Hospital. They paved the way for further change in the next two decades.

Notes

[1] Minutes of St Mark's PCC, 31 January 1973.

[2] Letter to the author from Michael Paton.

[3] Note of Annual Meeting on 23 April 1980.

[4] Minutes of St Mark's PCC, 10 September 1987.

[5] *Broomhill Magazine*, August 1971.

[6] *Flame*, February 1973.

[7] *Flame*, May 1973.

[8] *Broomhill Magazine*, September 1982.

[9] Minutes of St Mark's PCC, 6 February 1985, 4 June, 7 July and 11 September 1986; 9 January 1987.

[10] *Flame*, April 1973.

[11] Minutes of St Mark's PCC, 11 January, 17 January and 14 February 1978.

[12] Appendix to Gerald Levesley, *Third Jubilee – History of St George's Sheffield* (Sheffield: St George's PCC, 1975). Recollections of Roy Barry and Margaret Lyons.

[13] *Broomhill Magazine*, June 1978. Minutes of St Mark's PCC, 22 November 1979; 12 May 1980; 14 July 1980.

[14] Minutes of St Mark's PCC, 12 March and 12 September 1984.

[15] Minutes of St Mark's PCC, 15 July and 13 October 1987.

[16] Minutes of St Mark's PCC, 17 October 1974.

[17] Minutes of St Mark's PCC, 7 November 1985; 19 March, 4 June, 7 July and 11 September 1986; 9 January 1987.

[18] Minutes of St Mark's PCC, 6 February 1985.

[19] Minutes of St Mark's PCC, 21 October 1981' 8 September 1983; 17 October 1984; 5 September 1985; 26 February 1986.

[20] Minutes of St Mark's PCC, 25 May 1977; 11 January 1978; 26 February and 1 June 1981; 9 July 1985; 26 February 1986.

[21] Minutes of St Mark's PCC, 26 February and 9 July 1981.

[22] Minutes of St Mark's PCC, 27 June 1973 and 12 November 1973; 12 December 1978; 25 May 1982; 12 March 1984; 14 January 1988.

[23] Minutes of St Mark's PCC, 27 January 1982.

[24] Minutes of St Mark's PCC, 8 January and 19 March 1986.

[25] It had been loaned to St Silas in 1961 but in 1974 St Silas found it too expensive to maintain.

[26] Article by Jenny Dyson in *Flame*, August 1975.

[27] *Flame*, October 1973.

[28] Minutes of St Mark's PCC, 11 July and 18 September 1974.

[29] *Broomhill Messenger* Easter 1984. The *Broomhill Messenger* was an ecumenical newsletter distributed to homes in Broomhill at Christmas and Easter.

[30] Minutes of St Mark's PCC, 28 June 1973, 9 January and 14 March 1974.

[31] Minutes of St Mark's PCC, 17 March 1987; 14 January 1988.

[32] *Flame*, June 1975.

[33] Letter to the author from Michael Paton.

[34] Comment to the author by Ann Lewin.

[35] *Broomhill Magazine*, June 1978.

[36] Minutes of St Mark's PCC, 9 July 1981.

[37] Minutes of St Mark's PCC, 19 January and 28 November 1983.

[38] Minutes of Annual Meeting 27 April 1983.

[39] Minutes of St Mark's PCC, 12 September 1984.

[40] Minutes of St Mark's PCC, 19 March 1985.

[41] Minutes of St Mark's PCC, 30 April 1986.

[42] Minutes of St Mark's PCC, 9 January 1987.

[43] Letter to the author from John Giles.

[44] Minutes of Annual Meeting, 29 April 1987.

[45] PCC Minutes 10 September 1987.

CHAPTER 7

THE NINETIES AND THE NOUGHTIES
1988-2008

David Price

'It felt to me as if a huge padlock was being removed from a very solid looking door.' Jane Tillier on General Synod's vote in November 1992 to proceed with legislation to permit the ordination of women.[1]

'We have discovered our identity – re-established St Mark's in a liberal critical tradition, strengthened and stimulated by our groups, our conference and our quest for the historical Jesus.' Adrian Alker at St Mark's Annual Meeting, 23 April 2001.

In the late 1980s, St Mark's was a lively, open and tolerant church, attracting many people from beyond its parish boundaries. There were 130-140 communicants each Sunday, many committees and groups and good links with the local community. Beyond its local area, it was not particularly well known.

It was a difficult time for the Church of England. The movement for the ordination of women was gathering strength, but a minority of Anglicans was resolutely opposed to it. Church attendance was still shrinking. In 1988, it was agreed to launch a Decade of Evangelism in the 1990s, but the main effect of this was a 'reduced speed of church decline'.[2] Liberal Anglicanism certainly seemed in decline, while evangelicals were gaining in numbers and confidence.

Like the Church of England as a whole, St Mark's faced problems in achieving change. The previous Vicar, John Giles, had felt that the congregation was too divided into separate groups, each pursuing its own agenda. A Deanery report said that at St Mark's new ideas often 'died the death of a thousand qualifications'.[3] The beautiful church building needed adaptation to changing needs, but there was no consensus on how to use the church's considerable financial reserves.

This was the situation in 1988, when the Church Burgesses and the church wardens, Chris Knight and Margaret Lyons, chose Adrian Alker as the new Vicar. As he and his wife, Christine, will be well known to many readers, they are referred to throughout as Adrian and Christine.

Leadership

Adrian was born in Wigan in Lancashire. His family lived next door to an Anglican church in which he was involved from his earliest days. After studying history at Oxford, he became a careers officer for six years, before ordination training at Cuddesdon. He was parish priest in West Derby, Liverpool, and then a youth officer in the Diocese of Carlisle. As Vicar, he possessed persuasive charm, a rapport with young people, skill in talent spotting, abundant energy, imagination, idealism and a steely determination, which ensured that things never stood still, but could give rise to conflict when others saw things differently.

Adrian's wife, Christine, also did much for St Mark's, but sought to 'keep a low profile'.[4] The Alkers had a nine-year-old son, John, who quickly settled in Sheffield. Christine worked for a time in youth work training in Derbyshire, and then for many years as paid administrator at St Mark's, as well as playing a leading voluntary role in the church's youth work.

Since 1978, St Mark's had not had a curate, but Adrian wanted full-time support. Others, concerned about the cost, argued that retired clergy could provide the necessary help. But the Diocese saw St Mark's as offering good training opportunities for a curate. St Mark's benefited from the ministries of a succession of able women:

• 1991-95. Jane Tillier, a deacon, became curate in 1991 and was caught up in the drama of women's ordination. She later became Chaplain of Gloucester Cathedral.

77. John, Adrian and Christine Alker in 1988 (photograph courtesy of Cumbrian Newspapers Ltd).

• 1995-97. Hilary Jowett, was formerly Chaplain of Nether Edge Hospital. She later became Team Rector of Christ Church, Gleadless.

• 1997-2002. Jane Bolton, a former hospital administrator, came straight from Cuddesdon, and served initially as Curate and then from 2000 as Associate Vicar. In 2002, Jane became Rector of Dinnington and Laughton en le Morthen.

• 2002 - 2004. Sally Fairweather was formerly based at Holy Rood House, a Christian centre for health and pastoral care in Thirsk in North Yorkshire. In 2004, she joined Sheffield's mental health chaplaincy team.

• 2005-2009. Sue Hobley, a former secondary teacher, came from Washington in Tyne and Wear to be Assistant Priest, having already served in Sunderland as a curate. When Adrian left in 2008, she kept the church running during the interregnum. Then in 2009, she became Vicar of Wath upon Dearne.

Early on, Adrian received help from Michael Bayley until summer 1993, when Bayley became project leader at St Mary's, Bramall Lane. Adrian also had support from, and links with, university and health chaplains, notably John Earwaker (see fig 79). From 2002, Ian Maher CA assisted with preaching and worship. Retired clergy who contributed to the life of St Mark's included Vyvyan Watts-Jones, John Wood, Peter Fisher and Michael Page.

From 2000 to 2003, Noel Irwin, who combined Biblical scholarship with a Belfast accent and a strong social conscience, was lay worker, particularly in Broomhall.

There were at various times several Readers – David McClean, Gill Watts-Jones, Liz Chester, Peter Bolton (husband of Jane Bolton) and Michael Burn (husband of Sue Hobley). Church Wardens are listed in Appendix 1.

Diocese and Deanery

From 1989 to 1994, Adrian helped the Diocese with post-ordination training of clergy. At this time, the Diocese, led by Bishop David Lunn, was struggling financially, owing to the collapse of industry in South Yorkshire and the reduction in support from the Church Commissioners. The Diocese looked to churches like St Mark's in the prosperous Hallam Deanery for support. The Diocesan 'share' paid by St Mark's rose from £14,504 in 1989 to £76,754 in 2007 – three times the rate of inflation.

Alarming divisions were arising within the Diocese. As an Anglo-Catholic, David Lunn opposed the ordination of women to the priesthood, although there were 30 women deacons in his Diocese, mostly aspiring to become priests. The introduction of women priests caused 24 priests from the Diocese to join the Roman Catholic Church and one to become an Orthodox priest.[5] Lunn stayed in post and was fair-minded to ordained women, but he delegated their ordination to his suffragan.

In Hallam Deanery, the churchmanship of the three biggest churches diverged. St Mark's became more progressive. The conservative evangelical Christ Church, Fulwood, opposed the ordination of women. St Thomas, Crookes, continued to develop as a massive evangelical charismatic church, despite the sensational collapse of the Nine O'Clock Service in 1995. In 2003, it created the Philadelphia Campus. These three churches all drew many members from outside their parishes and built wider networks.

In 1997, Jack Nicholls became Bishop (see Figure 86 on page 96). Although Anglo-Catholic in background like Lunn, he fully accepted women priests.

Resource Problems

Soon after Adrian arrived, tensions over resources arose as a result of three factors: the growing Diocesan 'share', Adrian's plans for the church, and the 'donations policy' established in 1965, under which 20.5% of annual given income was donated to charity. This meant that new spending required an extra fifth for donations (for the origins of this policy, see page 68).

Adrian's starting point was to question whether St Mark's should be holding on to reserves worth over £113,000. In October 1989, he produced a radical three-pronged spending plan, embracing building improvements, the appointment of an assistant curate and a large donation to the new church of St Bartholomew's, Netherthorpe.[6] In January 1990, he won support for this plan at a Parish Gathering. We shall pursue the separate strands of Adrian's plan elsewhere. Here we look at the financial issues.

Given income did increase, but not sufficiently, and 1992 proved to be a 'traumatic year' financially.[7] By now, the church was committed to substantial extra expenditure, but income was flagging owing to the national recession. In June, Roy Godden, Church Treasurer, and David Ryder (then Church Warden but Treasurer from 1995) warned of a looming deficit of £6,000 and challenged the 'donations policy'. The Overseas Committee was unhappy. Adrian argued that the donations policy reflected Christ's concern for the poor and needy. But the PCC eventually decided to reduce donations, with Adrian alone voting against.[8]

Adrian found 1992 stressful, mainly because of this financial crisis. In the autumn, he even thought of resigning but by January 1993 he felt more settled and strongly affirmed by the church community.[9]

In 1993, it was agreed to base donations, still at 20.5%, on average congregational giving over the last two years.[10] In 1995, faced with increasing costs, Roy Godden and David Ryder again queried the donations policy. Following a review by a working party, the PCC decided to reduce donations to 15%.[11] In November 1999, Ryder's budget for 2000 showed a disturbingly large deficit, again partly due to Diocesan Share. Various economy measures were agreed, including a reduction in donations to 10%, backed on this occasion both by Adrian and Roy Barry of the International Committee.[12] Donations have remained at 10% ever since.

Worship

This was a time of experimentation in worship at St Mark's. The congregation was highly creative – musically and liturgically – and included many without an Anglican background. Adrian was eclectic in his search for forms of worship that would create a 'sense of mystery, awe and wonder'.[13]

The first major change was the introduction in October 1988 of a new service – the Prayer of Hope – at 8.00pm, using 'such stimuli as light and darkness, silence and chants' from Taizé. Adrian appreciated the spirituality of Taizé. He and Jonathan Clatworthy, Anglican University Chaplain, wanted a non-Anglican service that would appeal to students and could be led by them. This quiet reflective service has lasted to this day, known from 1996 as 'Night Service'.

Early in 1991, St Mark's introduced its own service book for the Parish Communion, including variations favoured at St Mark's. In 1997, there was a debate over incense, first used at Night Service in 1991 by Freddy Masole, an Anglo-Catholic priest from South Africa. Thereafter, Adrian used incense occasionally. Despite objections on doctrinal and health grounds, the PCC authorised its continued limited use.[14]

As Adrian felt that Parish Communion might not suit some young families, in October 1997 a monthly all-age service called 'Sunday Best' was introduced at 11.15am. Attendance ranged between 50 to 70, of whom half were children. Sunday Best continued until 2000, when children began to receive Communion (see below). Thereafter, there was an 'all age' communion service once a month accompanied by a band. This gave licence for less solemnity, as when Noel Irwin and Adrian wore pigs' masks and retold the parable of the prodigal son from the pigs' perspective.[15]

In 1999, the pattern of Sunday services changed. Parish Communion now started at 10.00am instead of 9.45am. Sunday Best continued monthly at 11.30am.[16] The 6.30pm evening service was dropped as it was too poorly attended. The 6.00pm slot was used for learning; for example, there was a six-part series on 'The Meaning of Jesus' in 1999. Night Service remained at 8.00pm.

There was much debate about liturgy. In 2000, *Common Worship* superseded the *Alternative Service Book*. The various Eucharistic Prayers were tried and H was preferred, but there was some criticism of *Common Worship* and suggestions that liturgists close to St Mark's, such as Jim Cotter and Janet Morley, should have been drawn into the drafting. Around this time, separate service sheets were introduced, as in Cathedrals and large parish churches. The difference at St Mark's was the willingness to use liturgies beyond those in *Common Worship*, derived from sources such as the Iona Community.

The Ordination of Women

St Mark's felt emotionally involved in the drama over women's ordination in the early 1990s. Not only was this a liberal cause. It was a St Mark's layman, David McClean, Chair of the House of Laity of General Synod, who master-minded the legislation. Furthermore, St Mark's' Curate, Jane Tillier, was closely affected.

Before Jane Tillier arrived, Maureen Whitebrook advised from experience at an American Episcopalian Church of the need to prepare for the 'difference' that women's ministry represented. A meeting, attended mainly by women, voted on women's ordination with 67 in favour, one against and 4 abstentions.[17]

Jane Tillier's charm, sincerity and ability soon won over any waverers. In 1992, there was anger when Jane Tillier could not be ordained alongside men who had become deacons with her. Adrian was '*deeply hurt* for her and the church'.[18] On Whit Sunday, he presided at a Eucharist for the Movement for the Ordination of Women (MOW). On 7 June, Anglia TV showed a programme called 'The Curate's Egg' featuring Jane Tillier. In October, there were nine days of prayer before the crucial General Synod debate on 11 November 1992, in which St Mark's played a significant part. Its former Vicar, Michael Adie, Bishop of Guildford, led off and wound up the day's debate on the proposal to move to legislation on women's ordination; David McClean re-opened the debate in the afternoon and moved the approval of the second measure and the related Canon. There was enormous relief (and some surprise) when this was approved by the necessary two-thirds majorities.

78. The Revd Jane Tillier (second from left) at her ordination in Sheffield Cathedral by the Rt Revd Michael Gear, Bishop of Doncaster, on 15 March 1994.

On 15 March 1994, Jane Tillier was ordained by Michael Gear, the Bishop of Doncaster. The following Sunday she presided for the first time at Parish Communion, with David McClean preaching. Experience with women's ordination intensified St Mark's commitment to inclusivity. Both Jane Tillier and her successor, Hilary Jowett, promoted inclusive language at St Mark's and this was reflected in the purchase of *Hymns Old and New* in 1996.

Human Sexuality

Further inclusivity issues were raised by the House of Bishops' 1991 report 'Issues in Human Sexuality', which ruled out 'active homophile partnerships' for clergy and called for 'a process of Christian reflection'. At St Mark's, this reflection genuinely took place. In May 1996, Adrian set the scene for a visit by the Revd Richard Kirker, General Secretary of the Lesbian and Gay Christian Movement (LGCM), by urging that the church should 'affirm loving faithful relationships both heterosexual and homosexual, whilst clearly speaking out against promiscuity, casual sex and oppression of the young'.[19]

In 1998, however, the Lambeth Conference rejected homosexual practice as incompatible with scripture and opposed the blessing or ordaining of those involved in same gender unions. There was a shocked reaction at St Mark's and nine members attended LGCM's Derby Conference in February 1999.[20] Adrian drafted a statement for the PCC, but at first agreement could not be reached.

On 1 July 2000, a church conference on 'Human Relationships' was held, attended by 50 people. It discussed not just homosexual relationships but also marriage, cohabitation, breakdown of relationships, divorce and remarriage. Subsequently, the PCC approved a leaflet entitled 'To Love and Cherish', which included the following statements:

- The community at St Mark's wishes to affirm a wide range of loving, faithful and committed relationships. ...

- Marriage after divorce may be possible; talk this through with a member of the clergy. …
- Some people have a deeply loving relationship with another person of the same sex.
- There may be a time when you seek to have this relationship blessed and offered to God in a service of commitment and thanksgiving. A member of the clergy will be able to talk this through with you and possibly help you plan such a service.[21]

In 2003 tension in the Anglican Communion intensified, when in the USA Gene Robinson, who was in a gay relationship, was elected Bishop of New Hampshire and in England Canon Jeffrey John was persuaded *not* to become Bishop of Reading. St Mark's was unusual in the Diocese in having open debate about these sensitive issues.

Music and Drama

St Mark's had an unusual range of musical and dramatic talent, but, soon after Adrian's arrival, there was a crisis over music. Bob Johnson had been organist and choirmaster for 27 years and trained the choir well, but several parents wanted their children to be able to join the choir. Johnson resisted this idea and eventually resigned. It was agreed to separate the roles of organist and music co-ordinator. Alan Brown, Lecturer in Music at Sheffield University, became organist. The post of music co-ordinator was advertised unsuccessfully, so in 1989 Janet Earwaker became music co-ordinator, working with Eve Saunders and Steve Draper as 'choir trainers'. All worked unpaid. Choir practice was at 9.00am on Sunday. Children joined the choir, practising on Thursday evening. In 1998, Peter Bolton took over as 'co-ordinator'.

The volunteer music team (now Janet Earwaker, Andrew Sanderson, David Sanderson and Eve Saunders) directed the choir until January 2004, when the Revd Gareth Green was briefly Music Minister. From September 2004 to 2009, Andy Thomas was Music Co-ordinator. As well as contributing to Parish Communion, the choir sang on Passion Sunday and at Advent works such as Britten's *Ceremony of Carols* (2004), Fanshawe's *African Sanctus*, in the presence of the composer (2005), and Bernstein's *Chichester Psalms* (2006). An Organ Scholarship was introduced in 2007 with Wendy Dickinson as the first Organ Scholar.

79. The Revd John Earwaker, Chaplain of Sheffield City Polytechnic (1981-92) and Sheffield Hallam University (1992-3). Inspired author and composer of *Cousin John*. (photograph: Janet Earwaker)

Meanwhile St Mark's tradition of musical drama, begun in 1986, continued, with Britten's *The Little Sweep* in 1989, two one-act operas in 1990 and Britten's *St Nicholas* in 1992. But the outstanding production was *Cousin John*, performed in June 1999 at the Merlin Theatre – a remarkable musical play by John Earwaker about John the Baptist, combining racy dialogue and catchy tunes. It was such a hit that a concert version was produced in 2003 and a second full-stage version at the Montgomery Theatre in June 2008 in memory of John Earwaker, who sadly died in 2007.

On Christmas Eve, the church continued the tradition started in 1979 of a nativity play based on a story such as Good King Wenceslas, followed by a tableau of Jesus' birth. Iain Strath wrote and produced these plays, which were much appreciated by children and their parents. On Shrove Tuesday, there was a satirical review about life at St Mark's.

80. Colin Brady as John the Baptist in *Cousin John*, together with his followers.

Children and Young People

Inclusion of children and young people in the church's life was an important theme. Activities included an Adventure Club, EAYOR (enter at your own risk), children's choir, Steeple People (teenagers) and Lions Drama, whose annual pantomime was hilarious. The clergy sought to involve children in worship. At the end of Parish Communion, children were invited to the Sanctuary to tell the congregation about their activities doing the service.

The biggest innovation was the admission of children to Communion. Adrian seized the opportunity of a period of church experimentation to bring children into the very heart of worship. He obtained Bishop Jack Nicholls' authority to admit baptised people of any age, including babes in arms, to Communion. On Passion Sunday 2000, Bishop Jack presided when 35 baptised children received Communion for the first time. In November 2000, the PCC agreed that confirmation should be offered to baptised people aged 16 and over. [22]

Much dedicated work with children continued. In 2007-8, the pattern on Sunday was the crèche, the Sunday Club for younger children and Lions for older children, including breakfast in the Vicarage. A PCC review noted a weakness in relation to 14-18 year olds. During the week, there was MADCats on Thursday evenings at St Mark's. Also on Thursdays was the (ecumenical) Youth Club, which moved in 2000 from St Mark's to Hanover Methodist

81. The Revd Sue Hobley, Associate Vicar from 2005 to 2009, and the children at the end of Parish Communion (photograph: David Stoker).

Church and then in 2007 to the Broomhall Centre. Led by Dilys Noble, this was 'an open club with a Christian basis in a multi-cultural and multi-faith community'. [23]

The Building

At Adrian's induction to his new job, Bishop David Lunn told him that he would be 'guardian of the shrine'. The 'shrine' needed modernising in a way that honoured its fine 1960s architecture. After a crisis in 1989 over asbestos in the building, major building improvements were planned. They were carried out in 1992. The choir vestry, cluttered with the frontal chest, was replaced by the new Church Lounge, accessible by two new doors from the narthex, together with a new kitchen, with the exterior wall pushed outwards. Additional toilet facilities were provided. The toilet adjoining the clergy vestry was sacrificed to make way for the frontal chest.

The project cost £87,000, funded from the proceeds of the sale of the church hall (to be recouped over the next 30 years) and the sale of the Mission Hall in Broomspring Lane and fabric reserves. Michael Adie, then Bishop of Guildford, opened the new facilities on 8 November 1992. The new lounge and kitchen soon proved their worth, transforming fellowship after Parish Communion and making possible the new lunch club for the elderly (see below) and many other functions, including facilities for the wider community and social spaces for large conferences.

In 1999, Beryl Jordan, former academic registrar and PCC Secretary, died, leaving St Mark's £150,000. She wanted £10,000 to be spent on 'the poor, sick and elderly' but the rest was to be used at the Vicar's discretion. This made possible a second building project – facilitating disabled access to the Upper Room by installing a lift, improving office accommodation, storage and toilet facilities, and expanding the Upper Room. Fire regulations required a new staircase, which meant removing some space and pews from the western end of the worship area. The Twentieth Century Society complained about tampering with a Grade 2 listed building, but did not press their objections. The cost of around £260,000 required the PCC again to use the church's investments and gradually to rebuild the reserves. [24] The work was completed in 2002. The subsequent redecoration of the church triggered a second asbestos crisis, requiring careful sealing of asbestos wall panels.

Adrian wanted to replace all the pews with chairs in order to create a more flexible space, but the cost and widespread preference for pews prevented this from happening. The front pews were made removable and chairs replaced fixed pews in the Chapel. Around 1995, David and Pamela McClean donated silver tips to the Church Wardens' staves in memory of David's father.

Other smaller projects undertaken in this period (often assisted by specific donations or legacies) were:

- the creation of the library in the narthex and later its extension;
- the joining up of the altar rail with two 'gates' installed;
- renewal of the church lighting;
- installing a Celtic cross in 1999 in the Garden of Remembrance, designed by Ronald Sims, who had been George Pace's partner;
- installation of pew runners (cushioned seating) in 2007;
- insulation of the Chapel ceiling;
- refurbishment of the tower louvres.

Pastoral Care

People at St Mark's saw the kingdom of God – Jesus' central theme – not as remote and heavenly but as here and now. Kingdom values guided the church's Pastoral Care Committee, supportive groups and visiting, and led to two important innovations:

- The employment of a part time pastoral worker – at first Ann Lentell and Audrey Mills jointly, then Audrey Mills on her own. In 1996-7, responsibility shifted to Churches Together in Broomhill and Anne Bryant was appointed 'worker with older people', succeeded in 2000 by Janet Brown, who served Broomhall as well as Broomhill.[25] This appointment was the first of its kind in the city. (See Figure 88 on page 97).

- The St Mark's Lunch and Friendship Club for elderly people living alone, launched in September 1992 and held every Wednesday in the new church lounge and kitchen. Into it was merged the long-established Ashgate Friendship Club. Anne Button, a lecturer in catering, took charge of fund-raising, training the committed team of volunteers and ensuring supplies. Community Transport was used. Lunch cost £1.50 and was followed by entertainment organised by Jennifer Powell or Rosalind Rogerson. Lunch was provided initially for about 20 people, but by 2006, 45 lunches were being produced.[26] Food, friendship and fellowship were offered to elderly people whose lives were very restricted.

St Mark's was prepared to offer pastoral care in the most terrible of circumstances, as in responding to the tragedy at Hillsborough Football Ground on 15 April 1989, in which 95 people lost their lives. Adrian suddenly found himself helping one of the bereaved from the church in Skelmersdale which his family attended. Thereafter, he and several lay colleagues from the congregation visited victims of the disaster in the Royal Hallamshire Hospital and offered support for a long time afterwards.

Social Responsibility

82. Anne Button, one of the founders of the Lunch Club, preparing the Christmas lunch in 2005.

Kingdom values also guided endeavours concerned with social responsibility. In February 1989, St Mark's formed a group on the Bishop's Appeal for St Bartholomew's, Netherthorpe. Eventually, St Mark's donated £20,000 from its reserves and £20,000 from individuals.[27] The group soon became the 'Faith in the City Task Force', then in 1992 the 'Social Responsibility Committee' (SRC), covering St Mark's response to social needs.[28] In 1992, homelessness, housing, poverty and unemployment were found to be the congregation's greatest concerns.

Archdeacon Stephen Lowe advocated 'community organising', an American radical movement in which faith communities and other groups in poor areas were 'empowered' to demand improvements in their conditions. Several meetings about this were held at St Mark's, but, when in 1996 the project, now called 'Impact', went ahead in Sheffield, St Mark's did not participate, owing to doubts about its theology, politics, accountability and the potential distraction from St Mark's needs. By contrast, St Mark's neighbour, St John's, Ranmoor, was fully engaged in the

83. A Lunch Club summer outing.

project. Impact operated for several years in Sheffield, its main legacy being the enhancement of provision in the city to help people with debt problems.

From 1992 to 1998, St Mark's 'twinned' with St Thomas, Wincobank, and St Margaret's, Brightside, a joint parish greatly affected by industrial decline. Joint services were held and prayer links made. Clothing and food were collected at St Mark's.

The church and many church members subscribed in 1999 to the Employment Bond for employment schemes in Sheffield and in 2006 to the Investment Bond for tackling debt problems.

Interest in the environment intensified: 21 May 2000 was designated 'less car Sunday'. In 2001-2, Kay Hudson, Church Warden and church gardener, secured St Mark's recognition as an 'eco-congregation' on the basis of three projects: a compost event, an eco-fashion parade and an eco-service. In 2006-7 Michael Bayley encouraged St Mark's to take up climate change as a make-or-break issue. Sixty people attended Lent 'Omega Courses' in 2007 and many campaigned to tighten up greenhouse gas targets in what became the Climate Change Act 2008.

From 2000 onwards, large numbers of asylum seekers were based in Sheffield, including some in Broomhall. St Mark's people campaigned about the destitution affecting many of them. Some Zimbabwean asylum seekers, Priviledge Thulambo and her daughters, Valerie and Lorraine, worshipped regularly at St Mark's. There was a shocked reaction in 2009 when they were suddenly arrested and threatened with deportation. St Mark's joined strongly in the successful campaign for their release.

In the early 1990s, the radical Methodist, the Revd Dr John Vincent, urged St Mark's people to 'get their hands dirty' in difficult projects. St Mark's probably seemed to him too theoretical. There was much campaigning and some practical action, though it was difficult to tackle such problems as beggars coming to the Vicarage and church. Nevertheless, in this period three major social action projects emerged, which are discussed elsewhere – the Lunch Club (1992), the Broomhall Breakfast (2001) and the Soup Run (2007).

International Links

St Mark's attracted many people from overseas and strongly supported Christian Aid.
In 1991, the Revd Freddy Masole, a 25-year-old assistant priest from a township in Soweto, spent

84. The Revd Freddy Masole and the Rt Revd Trevor Huddleston at St Mark's in 1991 (photograph: David Bocking for Sheffield Telegraph).

nine months at St Mark's. The climax of his visit came on 27 April 1992, when the Rt Revd Trevor Huddleston met him and spoke about South Africa to a packed church. In 1994, Adrian spent part of a sabbatical in South Africa, visiting Masole's parish in Soweto and other contacts. Unfortunately, he was mugged in Johannesburg. Then he learned that his father had died, so he returned home in haste.

In 1992, the International Fellowship began. It met on the first Friday of each month for a shared meal, shared fellowship, a game of Jenga and a quiet meditative ending. It continued for nearly 20 years, bringing together people from across the world, sealing wonderful friendships and raising awareness of the needs of so many. For Adrian, this Fellowship was important witness to the table fellowship of Christ.

85. The game of Jenga was regularly played at the International Fellowship's monthly shared meal (photograph: Beryl Barry).

Through Hobson Nnebe, St Mark's formed a link with St Christopher's Church, Kaduna, in Northern Nigeria. Four St Mark's people visited to Kaduna in 1996, and five Kaduna people came to Broomhill in 1999. Unfortunately, the link was difficult to maintain because of communications problems, clergy changes at St Christopher's and religious violence in Northern Nigeria.

Three other overseas links emerged from within the congregation:

- Moises Pedraza and Mary Luz from Colombia, having worshipped at St Mark's, set up a charity in Bogota working with street children. SUCCOL was formed to raise funds for this work. Adrian and Christine Alker visited Bogota in 2003.
- John Bramley's sister, Susan, launched a charity called the Sakhelwe Trust, combatting HIV/AIDS in South Africa, which St Mark's supported.
- Dilys Noble helped with aid to needy children in Romania.

The Trust formed from a bequest by Professor Mainland in 1988[29] helped several young people to travel to developing countries.

Finally, the International Committee encouraged campaigning on issues around trade justice, including the Jubilee Debt Campaign and 'Make Poverty History'. At the time of the G8 Summit in May 1998, many of the congregation joined the human chain of 70,000 people in Birmingham as part of Jubilee 2000.

Broomhill

Adrian strongly believed in the parish church's 'role in the community'. He gave high priority to the Broomhill Festival every June and chaired the Festival Committee for 19 years. The Festival became the biggest suburban festival in Sheffield, and the money it raised for charity increased from £3,000 in 1995 to £17,000 in 2007. The annual Garden Party on St Mark's Green was always a big event for St Mark's. The Festival was very dependent on St Mark's, but also highlighted the opportunities that the eclectic congregation had to reach out to the parish of Broomhill. There were great rewards, in marking out the church's commitment to good causes and service to its community. The contribution of St Mark's university students was outstanding and served to deepen their friendships and commitment to the church.

Adrian was also Chair of the Broomhill Forum for ten years. He was respected in Broomhill as someone who could bring differing voices together to help resolve conflict arising from issues related, for example, to traffic, the licensing of public houses and the University's Student Village.

86. Bishop Jack Nicholls and his wife Judith judge the fancy dress competition at the Broomhill Festival Garden Party in 2004 (photograph: Adrian Alker).

Broomhall

From 1859 to 1991, the parish was known as 'St Mark's Broomhall', although from 1961 Broomhall was completely outside the Parish (see Chapter 5). In 1991, at Adrian's suggestion, a pastoral order was obtained changing the title of the parish to 'St Mark's Broomhill', as the church had in fact been known for years, but in 1999 Archdeacon Stephen Lowe informed Adrian of the dissolution of the parish of St Silas, which meant that the area west of the ring road became part of St Mark's parish and the rest went to St Matthew's, Carver Street (see map at Figure 71 on page 76). St Silas Church was sold to the YMCA.

This was a challenge for St Mark's. Broomhall was different from Broomhill. Many of its 3,000 population were unemployed or otherwise disadvantaged. They were ethnically very mixed, with a large and growing Somali population. But a way forward was agreed. Jane Bolton would stay longer as Associate Vicar and St Mark's would have a lay outreach worker in Broomhall.

In 2000, Noel Irwin was recruited as the outreach worker, living in Broomhall in a flat attached to Hanover Methodist Church. St Mark's made a covenant with Hanover Methodist Church, under which Jane Bolton presided at an Anglican Eucharist there once a month. Janet Stafford, a

87. St Silas Church, Broomhall, in 2013. Its closure in 2000 led to an expansion of St Mark's parish into Broomhall.

Methodist deacon, was based at Hanover. It was a strong team.

Jane Bolton and Noel Irwin became very familiar with this small but diverse area. Both joined the Broomhall Forum. Jane Bolton took a course in basic Somali and got to know some of the Somali women. Noel studied community work and in 2001 established the Broomhall Breakfast on Friday mornings at Hanover Methodist Church. It was open to all, whether homeless or vulnerable or hungry on their way to work. He later commented: 'It is wonderful to see street drinkers sitting around a table with university lecturers chatting and for me this says something very profound about what being church is.'[30] He also developed a Credit Union outlet.

Noel Irwin, Jane Bolton and her two successors, Sally Fairweather and Sue Hobley, devoted much energy to Broomhall, but things became more difficult. In 2003, Noel left for Victoria Hall Methodist Church. The YMCA's plans for the St Silas building stalled and eventually the YMCA put the building up for sale. Nor was there progress towards a full ecumenical project with a joint minister.[31] Janet Stafford left and was not replaced.

In July 2007, Ecclesall Methodist Circuit decided to close Hanover Methodist Church, selling it to the Jesus Fellowship Church (Jesus Army). St Mark's had lost its base in Broomhall. St Andrew's URC was nearby, friendly and helpful, and housed the weekly Breakfast. But overall, the problems

created by extending St Mark's parish into Broomhall were not fully resolved. Some St Silas people had moved to Hanover Methodist Church, but few went to St Mark's. Sue Hobley comments that St Mark's had few people of a working-class background: 'very few non-professional people who lived in Broomhall made the journey up the hill to worship at St Mark's when the parishes merged. It may have felt quite intimidating.'[32]

88. Janet Brown, the churches' worker with older people, and one of the breakfasters at the Broomhall Breakfast (photograph: Sarah Hall).

Students

St Mark's was close to the Anglican Chaplaincy at Sheffield University. Linda Kirk chaired its governing body, on which others from the congregation also served. Jonathan Clatworthy, Anglican Chaplain, was on the staff of St Mark's until he left in 1991. There were also links with Sheffield City Polytechnic (from 1992 Sheffield Hallam University - SHU). John Earwaker continued there as Anglican Chaplain until 1993, when he retired following a heart attack. In 2006, this link was resumed when a member of St Mark's, Ian Maher CA, became SHU's Multi-Faith Chaplaincy Co-ordinator.

The church's involvement with students fluctuated, with only one student attending in 1988.[33] In 1997, Gary Grief, working with students, commented: 'All the halls (of residence) have their own Christian Unions which do not recognise St Mark's as a "sound" church.'[34] Adrian wondered how many students wanted 'a church which is unsettling because it is engaged in that exciting but rather turbulent pursuit of truth'.[35]

St Mark's work with students was sometimes led by members of the congregation and sometimes by student workers, who included Ali Burdon, Sarah Glasswell, Andy Thomas and Tess Keeble. Night Service proved particularly attractive to students.

A buoyant period for students began in 2002. Many went to Taizé with Sally Fairweather for the New Year. Alistair Sutcliffe became student representative on the PCC. By September 2004, student numbers were rising more than at any time before[36] and 20-30 students were actively integrated into the church, doing work with children, serving at the Eucharist and coming to Night Service, and helping with the Broomhill Festival. Many stayed at St Mark's for years and even found their marriage partners there.

In October 2005, Andy Thomas became student worker as well as music co-ordinator. A lively programme resulted, with a weekly evening gathering called 'The Space', which included a meal.

89. The Broomhill Festival student team and members of the Festival Committee celebrate another great five-a-side soccer tournament in June 2006, when medals were awarded by Cllr Jackie Drayton, Lord Mayor of Sheffield (photograph by David Stoker).

Controversial discussions were organised at Coffee Revolution on themes such as 'Why it is OK to be Christian and gay'.

In 2007, two students, Jez Thomas and Lucy Dunlop, suggested providing a Soup Run for homeless and vulnerable people at 6.30pm on Saturdays to fill a gap in the churches' programme of nightly soup runs. This was approved by the PCC and a rota of students and others was formed. The soup run continues to this day.

Holding the Congregation Together

Like his predecessors, Adrian sought ways of integrating the large congregation. In 1988, Pam McClean's review of communications led to the launch of *Mark's Messenger*, a new parish magazine, which Pam and her husband edited for the first few years. 'Welcome Teams' continued to greet people coming to Parish Communion. Photographs of members of the congregation were posted in the lounge to help people to get to know each other. There were regular congregational gatherings, known as Parish Days. In April 1994, a Parish Weekend was held at Cliff College, led by the Bishop of Jarrow and Roly Bain, a clerical clown, and attended by 125 people. In 2006, another Parish Weekend was held at the Hayes, Swanwick, attended by 130 people. St Mark's also launched its own website around 2002. Christian hospitality was emphasised, with Sunday lunch open to all and well attended.

The rich range of groups linked to St Mark's continued, involving large numbers of people. There was an increasing emphasis on radical theology (see below) and later on ecological issues.

In January 2002, Canon Mike West led a seminar to discern church vocation. St Mark's strengths were seen as inclusivity/tolerance, friendly welcome and interest in theology. The church needed to consider further: the balance between 'theological adventurism' and traditional worship, the needs of Broomhall and St Mark's role as a gathered church responsible for a defined geographical area.[37] The number of people on the electoral roll who lived in the parish in fact declined from 34% in 2000 to 24% in 2008. (In 2013, the proportion was also 24%.)[38]

90. Members of the congregation attending the Parish Weekend
at the Hayes, Swanwick, in September 2006.

Ecumenism and Inter Faith

From the mid 1980s, St Mark's relationship with the Methodists was weakened because Broomhill Methodists were worshipping at Carver Street Methodist Church, but in 1995 the Methodists decided to sell their historic Carver Street building and pushed ahead with their new church on the old Wesley site in Broomhill.[39] At last, in February 1998, the new Broomhill Methodist Church opened.

The Methodists' return to Broomhill strengthened ecumenical links. Adrian, Jonathan Kerry,

Methodist Minister, and Fleur Houston, Minister at St Andrew's URC, worked closely together and, on 24 January 1999, with lay colleagues, launched Churches Together in Broomhill (CTB), with Donald Smith as first Moderator.

In 2000, CTB was replaced by CTBB (Churches Together in Broomhill and Broomhall), as St Mark's Parish extended into Broomhall and Hanover Methodist Church was included. On Good Friday 2000, 70 people joined a Walk of Witness from Broomhill Methodist Church to Hanover, via St Mark's and St Andrew's. The founders of CTBB were keen on community action, so various projects became

91. The launch of Churches Together in Broomhill on 24 January 1999. L to R: Adrian, Jenny Carpenter, the Revd Jonathan Kerry, Donald Smith and the Revd Fleur Houston (photograph: Donald and Josey Smith).

CTBB projects – the worker with older people, the Broomhall Breakfast and the Broomhall youth club.

An inter-faith dimension at St Mark's was new and took the form of a relationship with Severn Road Mosque. From 1993 onwards, there were Christian-Muslim dialogues. Adrian worked closely with Abdool Gooljar, then playing a leading role at the mosque. During the First Gulf War people from St Mark's joined in a walk from the mosque to St Mark's and another similar walk took place on the first anniversary of 9/11.[40]

Radical Theology and the Centre for Radical Christianity

Adrian's ministry later became notable for its theological radicalism, but on arrival he did not appear particularly radical theologically. His ideas and emphases developed during his 20 years at St Mark's. In the late 1980s, the most radical voices at St Mark's were two retired clergy – Vyvyan Watts-Jones and John Wood. Watts-Jones introduced the congregation to Matthew Fox's creation spirituality and Don Cupitt's *'Sea of Faith'* (though someone in the congregation described the latter as 'those three terrible words').[41] Watts-Jones died in June 1997.

In 1997, John Wood introduced Adrian to 'Meeting Jesus Again for the First Time' by Marcus Borg, a member of the 'Jesus Seminar' of American Biblical scholars.[42] Having read this book, Adrian wrote:

> I have recently been listening to a number of people at St Mark's who are more and more dissatisfied with the packaging of faith in propositional statements like the creeds or indeed in the kind of 'alpha courses' where there are right and wrong answers.... Where is there a place for doubt, for serious questioning, for more lateral thinking, for emptying?[43]

At this point, Adrian's theology became more radical. Borg's book became the basis for study groups involving over 50 people. In July 1998, Adrian came back from the Annual Conference of the Modern Churchpeople's Union inspired by the American Bishop Jack Spong. Adrian wrote: 'I believe St Mark's can and must be the kind of church to challenge complacency and to encourage everyone in the pursuit of God's truth.'[44] He highlighted Spong's book *Why Christianity Must Change or Die* at the Parish Day on 28 November and noted that 'Many people are excited by this challenge, some are anxious.'[45] Some people were unhappy with the sermons.[46] In 1997-8, Adrian encouraged radical questioning among the congregation through '3M (Third Millennium) groups'.

There was then a series of major conferences. In launching these, Adrian envisaged St Mark's becoming 'a centre for exploration and teaching' for 'open-minded' Christians over a wide area. For speakers, he drew mostly on American theologians, arguing that 'whilst we in this country were becoming more orthodox once more, across the Atlantic were many scholars looking again at the possibility of reconstructing the historical Jesus, with profound consequences for faith and doctrine'.[47] Adrian invited Marcus Borg to speak in December 2000, along with John Rogerson, Sheffield's leading Biblical scholar, much loved at St Mark's. Borg was witty, eloquent and learned, distinguishing sharply between 'the Jesus of history' and 'the Christ of faith'. For Adrian, the Conference was 'one of the most important events of (my) ministry. (It) ... brought together people with a similar view to the exploration of the historical Jesus and Marcus Borg had been a most charming guest.'[48]

Adrian wrote enthusiastically about the conference in the *Diocesan News*. In an article headed 'Best-seller Borg Wows Broomhill', he argued that Borg's popularity in the USA arose from the fact that he was a 'convinced believer ... a man who holds to a deep sense of the presence of God and values mystical experience, but who can eagerly debunk much classic Christian orthodoxy, on doctrines such as virgin birth, physical resurrection and dogmas of atonement.' This triggered a remarkable debate in the columns of *Diocesan News*. Several correspondents deplored any intellectualising that diverged from the Bible. Some said that they would be unable to disseminate *Diocesan News* in future if it contained 'heresy' and called upon the two bishops to proclaim the historic Gospel afresh. Liberals counter-attacked, fearing that 'the shrill voice of anti-intellectualism (would) drown out the quiet voice of serious scholarship' and alienate many from the church. Some who had attended the Conference pointed out that there had been a genuine sharing of views, with Professor Rogerson offering a critique of Borg's position and a variety of voices heard in discussion. The editor then closed the correspondence.[49]

In May 2001, Bishop Jack Nicholls spent a day in St Mark's parish and met the PCC. He saw St Mark's as 'a place where people can still be searching, on a journey'. 'St Mark's wants to be an inclusive church, but can be perceived from outside to be exclusive. But there is variety in the congregation, both in their background and how they believe.' He noted that

> the two biggest churches in the Diocese (Fulwood and St Thomas) ... influence the life of the diocese. However, the church is broad enough for people to differ. Smaller struggling churches need the knowledge that there is a strong questioning church in the diocese ... (St Mark's) can provide a resource for smaller churches ...[50]

Adrian reflected: 'St Mark's is not always held in high esteem by other parishes, but the Bishop had affirmed our work. We may be a thorn in people's sides, but we are necessary.'[51]

The second conference, in November 2001, attended by 250 people, was led by John Dominic Crossan, also from the Jesus Seminar. The PCC reflected that St Mark's was now seen as 'something of a flagship for the liberal/radical end of the church ... there is a network of people who look to St Mark's (and others) to keep them alive on their journey, when they are not being 'fed' in other ways...'[52]

Some felt that Adrian was moving too fast, when, for instance, he challenged the congregation to think critically about the nature of miracles as told in the Gospels. But he insisted that 'we will still tolerate a wide range of beliefs and opinions and ... everyone's journey and discipleship is honoured'.[53]

In October 2002, the third annual conference was led by Bishop Jack Spong. But not all the theological radicals who were drawn to Mark's came from across the Atlantic. In 2003, the church welcomed back an old friend whose links with St Mark's went back to 1976 – the Rt Revd David Jenkins, former Bishop of Durham.

At this point, Adrian saw a need for consolidation and he suggested setting up 'the St Mark's

Centre for Radical Christianity', self-financing and slightly separate from St Mark's, led by people 'committed to the cause of re-visioning the Christian faith for this new millennium', supported by St Mark's but 'not committing everyone who comes to St Mark's to nailing their colours to a Liberal mast'.[54] The PCC agreed and in July 2003 the Council of this new Centre was formed. Jane Padget was Chair, Helen Fisher Vice Chair, Robin Saunders Treasurer and Adrian Secretary. Marcus Borg and John Vincent were Patrons. The launch was at the fourth annual conference led by Bishop Richard Holloway, former Primus of the Scottish Episcopal Church. Already the CRC had 120 members. [55]The 'Object' was 'to support and help individuals and groups who are working towards prophetic, inclusive and open minded churches, unafraid to ask the big questions and committed to sharing Jesus' radical message of love and justice in their communities'.

92. The Rt Rev David Jenkins, former Bishop of Durham, visits St Mark's in 2003. L to R: Noel Irwin (lay outreach worker living in Broomhall, later Superintendent of Victoria Hall Methodist Church, Sheffield), Adrian, David Jenkins and the Revd Sally Fairweather, Associate Vicar.

St Mark's also joined PCN (Progressive Christianity Network) Britain, with Adrian on its management committee. PCN's eight points went on display in the church. In August 2004, Adrian hosted a meeting of representatives of progressive Christian organisations to explore an umbrella grouping of these bodies. The conclusion was positive but it would take time. In 2005, a course called 'Living the Questions' was introduced, featuring some of those who had spoken at the conferences.

St Mark's CRC continued to hold several events a year with high profile speakers, including Elizabeth Templeton, Robert Beckford, Keith Ward, Kenneth Leech, Gordon Lynch and Don Cupitt and reappearances of Borg, Crossan and Spong. After Spong's second visit in September 2005, he wrote to Adrian saying that St Mark's was 'the most exciting church I have met with in the UK'.[56]

93. Marcus Borg and the Council of St Mark's Centre for Radical Christianity in 2008. L to R. Front row: Anne Padget, Jane Padget, Tanya Ralph, Professor Marcus Borg, Helen Fisher, Anne Wood, Adrian Alker. Back row: Pauline Miller, Robin Saunders, Robin Story, David Thorpe and Jonny Wood.

Conclusion

In 2008, Adrian left St Mark's after 20 years to become Director of Mission Resourcing in the Diocese of Ripon and Leeds. Most of the congregation could remember no one other than him and Christine at the Vicarage. Adrian and Christine had worked with many able people – clergy and laity – to achieve a great deal, including major improvements to the building, stimulating work with children, young people, students and people from overseas, the enriching of worship and liturgy, the incorporation of Broomhall (even if leaving unfinished business), new social projects and new ecumenical relationships. Numbers are an elusive test. At a time of shrinking in the Church of England at large, Sunday communicants rose from 135 in 1988 to an average of 150 in 2008, but the comparison is confused by the admission of children to Communion from 2000. What is clear is that more people were coming to St Mark's on Christmas Eve and at other Festivals, on Sunday evenings for Night Service and during the week for all sorts of events, religious and secular. Early morning Holy Communion according to the Book of Common Prayer remained as an example of St Mark's inclusivity.

Most striking of all was the emergence of the St Mark's Centre for Radical Christianity, giving St Mark's a national profile for its theological exploration. This was not welcome to everyone in the Diocese, but Adrian's standing was recognised in 2005, when he became an Honorary Canon of Sheffield Cathedral.

In 2001-2, Chris Harrington, an evangelist in training in the Church Army, explored the 'unlikely notion of liberal evangelism' at St Mark's. He concluded that it was 'an open, welcoming, questioning, caring, community church in the Anglican tradition'.[57]

Notes

[1] *Mark's Messenger*, January 1993.

[2] Leslie Francis, Patrick Laycock and Andrew Village in 'Statistics for Evidence-Based Policy in the Church of England: Predicting Diocesan Performance', *Review of Religious Research* 52 (2), December 2010, pp. 207-20.

[3] Quoted by Adrian Alker in a letter of 24 January 1990, presumably referring to a visit by the Revd Michael Jarratt and the Deanery Pastoral Resource Team in 1984 (Minutes of St Mark's PCC, 18 July 1984).

[4] Profile by Diana Merrills. *Mark's Messenger*, May 1994.

[5] *Sheffield Diocesan News*, February 1996.

[6] Paper of 7 October 1989, 'Finance and Resources: A Strategy for the 1990s'.

[7] Roy Godden. Minutes of St Mark's PCC, 17 March 1993.

[8] Minutes of St Mark's PCC, October 1992, and Standing Committee, 20 October 1992.

[9] *Mark's Messenger*, January 1993.

[10] Minutes of St Mark's PCC, 10 February 1993.

[11] Minutes of St Mark's PCC, 8 February, 17 May, 14 September and 9 October 1995.

[12] Minutes of St Mark's PCC, 9 and 30 November 1999.

[13] *Mark's Messenger*, March 1995.

[14] Minutes of St Mark's PCC, 5 February 1997.

[15] *Mark's Messenger*, May 2001.

[16] Minutes of St Mark's PCC, 8 November 1996 and 20 July 1999.

[17] *Mark's Messenger*, January and April 1991.

[18] *Mark's Messenger*, June/July 1992.

[19] *Mark's Messenger*, May 1996.

[20] Minutes of St Mark's PCC, 20 May 1998 and 11 February 1999. *Mark's Messenger*, May 1998.

[21] Paper on Human Relationships. September 2000. Minutes of St Mark's PCC, 10 January, 11 July, 3 September and 3 October 2001. Pink leaflet 'To Love and to Cherish' with PCC papers.

[22] *Mark's Messenger*, January 2001. St Mark's leaflet: 'Children and Holy Communion'.

[23] David Gilks in St Mark's Annual Report, April 2008, p. 16.

[24] Minutes of St Mark's PCC, 10 October 2000, 5 December 2000, 6 November 2001, 3 February 2001, 3 and 10 December 2001, 1 September 2002 and 14 October 1992.

[25] *Mark's Messenger*, November 1990. Minutes of St Mark's PCC, 9 November 1993, 4 December 1995, 10 March 1997, 6 December 1999 and 23 February 2003.

[26] Minutes of St Mark's PCC, 12 November 1991, 8 June 9912, 16 September 1992 and 9 December 1992. *Mark's Messenger*, October 1992, March and April 1993.

[27] Minutes of St Mark's PCC, 9 November 1989.

[28] Note of meeting on 6 April 1992.

[29] Minutes of St Mark's PCC, 11 October 1988.

[30] St Mark's Annual Report, 2002.

[31] Author's note of meeting on 2 June 2004.

[32] Letter to author.

[33] Information from Adrian Alker.

[34] Minutes of St Mark's PCC, 8 October 1997.

[35] *Mark's Messenger*, September 1998.

[36] Alker's paper on staffing September 2004.

[37] Note from Mike West of 31 January 2002, on PCC file.

[38] Statistics presented by Electoral Roll Officer at Annual meeting.

[39] Minutes of St Mark's PCC, 21 March 1995 and 17 January 1996.

[40] .Information from Adrian Alker.

[41] *Mark's Messenger*, September 1994.

[42] *Mark's Messenger*, November 1997.

[43] *Mark's Messenger*, November 1997.

[44] *Mark's Messenger*, August 1998.

[45] *Mark's Messenger*, September 1998.

[46] Minutes of St Mark's PCC, September 1998.

[47] *Mark's Messenger,* Christmas 2001.

[48] Minutes of St Mark's PCC, 5 December 2000.

[49] *Sheffield Diocesan News*, February, March and April 2001.

[50] Minutes of St Mark's PCC, 21 May 2001.

[51] Minutes of St Mark's PCC, 21 May 2001.

[52] Minutes of St Mark's PCC, 3 December 2001.

[53] *Mark's Messenger*, Christmas 2001.

[54] *Mark's Messenger*, December 2002/January 2003.

[55] Minutes of St Mark's PCC, 15 January, 14 May, 22 January 13 October and 11 November 2003. *Mark's Messenger*, November 2003.

[56] *Mark's Messenger,* October 2005.

[57] *Mark's Messenger,* February 2002.

CHAPTER 8

A LIVING THINKING FAITH –
ST MARK'S TODAY

Michael Hunt

Adrian Alker's successor, appointed in 2009 after a nationwide advertisement, was the Revd Dr Ian Wallis, an energetic and scholarly priest whose previous appointments included the Chaplaincy of Sidney Sussex College, Cambridge, and eleven years as a parish priest in the north-east of England. Immediately prior to his appointment to St Mark's he had been Director of the Northern Ordination course in Wakefield. Coincidentally, both he and his wife Liz had been brought up in Sheffield - Ian had attended King Edward VII School across the road from St Mark's Green.

Ian's acute mind and eagerness to engage both academically and practically with key issues facing society in general (especially problems faced by the poor and marginalised) and the Church of England in particular (for example the continuing debates about the appointment of women to the episcopate and the blessing of civil partnerships) resonated with many members of the congregation. His capacity to draw on Biblical sources (and to interpret critically the meaning of these sources to help inform attitudes to contemporary issues) has been greatly valued. At an early stage in his ministry he suggested that St Mark's might do rather more to appear welcoming and inclusive and expressed concern about the visibility of St Mark's as a parish church. Whilst many people travelled up and down Glossop Road as they went about their daily lives, relatively few might be aware of the church or where it stood theologically. Even fewer might feel drawn to come in or be aware of the kind of welcome they would receive. As part of the response to this, the website was reorganised and expanded to provide a broader and much deeper understanding of the various activities of the church. Larger notice boards were placed around the boundaries of the church, also proclaiming its recently agreed expression of purpose - 'Living Thinking Faith'.

Sue Hobley had ably led St Mark's during the interregnum following Adrian's departure but it was inevitable that the diocese would soon wish to offer her a parish of her own and in 2009 she was appointed Vicar of Wath upon Dearne. In 2010, Ian was joined by the effervescent and thoughtful Sue Hammersley as Associate Vicar with particular responsibility for work in Broomhall. Her background in community work in Nottingham and experience of running a volunteer programme for young people were a valuable asset to the church. She also brought a much needed vitality to the work with younger people. Also in 2010, Shan Rush, a quietly perceptive paediatric nurse at the Children's Hospital, joined the ministry team as non-stipendiary deacon. (She was to be ordained to the priesthood in 2012.) St Mark's thus had a very strong clerical team complemented, as ever, by active 'retired' and associated clergy. In addition, a lay reader (Anne Padget) was licensed in 2012.

But what is the nature of St Mark's in 2013? What is its purpose and for whom does it exist? Previous chapters have drawn attention to the organic development of St Mark's since the parish was first created in the nineteenth century, and its evolution over the past 50 years into a church community firmly rooted in the liberal critical tradition. However a critical church must, at least occasionally, take the opportunity to review its purpose and mission. Ian Wallis has encouraged St Mark's to consider these issues and to provide some appropriate answers, as indicated by the priorities agreed by the PCC in February 2012. These included 'to nurture and grow an inclusive, accessible church community ... informed by liberal/progressive approaches to Christian faith …' and 'To support members of the congregation in their Christian discipleship … '.[1] Whilst the priorities may seem broad, they fit within the focus of a living thinking faith, the practical expression

94. Ian Wallis celebrating Holy Communion on Christmas Day 2012, with Sue Hammersley on his left and Shan Rush on the right. The servers are Richard Taylor and David Armstrong (photograph: Tanya Ralph).

of which provides the focus for this chapter. In attempting to understand what this means for 'St Mark's Today' members of the congregation were invited to provide their own views on what it was that attracted them to St Mark's, how they perceived recent changes and (in brief) the issues that the church should be addressing in the future. These views have been incorporated into this chapter.

St Mark's and Community

For a number of respondents, the fact that St Mark's is their parish church, with all the associated responsibilities expected of the established church, provides sufficient justification for worshipping here. Traditionally, of course, communities have developed around their local church with the daily and weekly pattern of worship offering an opportunity to look beyond the concerns of everyday life and to reflect on a vision of a different way of living, both individually and corporately. At the same time, the church and its community offer a refuge for those in need. It is clearly important that some (at least) of those worshiping in the parish church are familiar with the immediate geographical environment and conversant with its needs, and accept a responsibility to respond to them. But St Mark's also offers more than this. As one person pointed out, it is 'a parish church in the best sense in that it welcomes people of many shades of thought and does not identify itself exclusively with any narrow brand of church opinion'. There are thus no particular expectations of credal doctrines, nor does the church cling to particular rituals purely for historical reasons.

The welcome and the acceptance of diversity were also noted by many others in their replies and are clearly very strong features of the church. One church member wrote 'I ...value that I am allowed to be myself'. Another noted:

What I have always valued about St Mark's, and still do today, are the people who make up the [church] community, who work and struggle together, sharing their doubts, fears, pain, sufferings and joys and who attempt to follow Jesus' example of unconditional love for all.....

Another respondent recorded: 'The support and care from everyone here – being held in love by a huge community - is ... unique.' That St Mark's is a strong community is undoubted. This is reflected in its members' attachment to the church's open and questioning approach to theological issues as well as through their support for each other. Inevitably, this carries dangers. Is it a community that is difficult to break into? Is the 'openness' quite as permeable as we would wish to believe or does it exclude some who value certainty and continuity rather than ambiguity in their worship? Moreover, whilst St Mark's was able to absorb the congregation of the former University (and parish) church of St George's when it closed in 1978, it has been much less successful in attracting people from the parish of St Silas in Broomhall since the latter closed in 2000, with most of the parish being absorbed into an expanded parish of St Mark's (see Chapter. 7). It is also interesting in this context to reflect on the reasons why St Mark's has a significantly smaller congregation than either of the principal evangelical churches in the city, both of which attract substantially more university students to their services. Size alone, of course, is not important, but this relatively limited success in attracting young people who might be expected to be receptive to new ideas, approaches and understandings of the Christian gospel, coupled with less traditional liturgies, remains a cause for concern. Despite the appointment of a student worker and linkages with both university chaplaincies, it remains the case that many undergraduates arriving in the city as practising Christians seem to locate themselves with the more evangelical churches rather than with St Mark's.

As a parish church, St Mark's faces a dilemma because it serves a number of communities. First, the geographical parish, itself socially and economically diverse, which inevitably has changed substantially from the parish described in the earliest chapters of this book. Second, the community of people who are drawn to worship here, of whom at least two thirds live outside the parish. Third, not least as a result of the success of the Centre for Radical Christianity, it represents both to the diocese and to the country at large an example of a liberal critical church only rarely found elsewhere. The somewhat introspective debate about what it means to be a parish church in the twenty-first century, and thus where the priorities of a church such as St Mark's should lie in the future, is necessary and likely to continue into the foreseeable future.

Thinking Faith

The 2010 parish profile, revised to assist in the recruitment of a new Associate Vicar, summarised St Mark's position:

> We see faith as a journey. We read the Bible seriously but not literally and try to face up to the intellectual dilemmas facing thinking Christians today. We are committed to ecumenism, look for greater unity of the churches and consider inter-faith dialogue as important for our world today.[2]

This perception was reflected in the responses to the 2012 survey of the reasons why individual members of the congregation were attracted to St Mark's. Many respondents expressed gratitude for the opportunity to question some of the tenets of the Church (expressed for example in some of the creeds) and for the realisation that others shared their doubts and uncertainties about some of these (apparently) core tenets. A number of responses referred to a supportive, non-judgemental, community where people are encouraged to be themselves. One response in particular noted that 'some of the people from whom I have learned the most and whose opinions and judgements have influenced me the most, have come from St Mark's'. Another noted

It is a church where there is an absence of nonsense. It does not peddle certainty and answers and paradoxically it is the more convincing for that. It is a place where Christian agnostics can find a home alongside those who practise lives of traditional devotion.

The sense of a shared journey of faith where all have insights to offer and no one has a monopoly of truth was reflected very strongly in the responses. So too was a sense of excitement about the journey; that the search for a living faith could never be dull when there was so much more to be discussed or discerned. A number commented on the value of 'probing sermons' underpinned by high standards of scholarship, and the availability of sermons on the website, to be downloaded for further consideration and reflection, was clearly welcomed by many.[3] A complementary comment in the 2010 Worship Survey drew attention to

The on-going struggle to be theologically honest. The atmosphere of attentiveness. The reason I still find preaching at St Mark's alarming is that people appear to listen and then comment and discuss afterwards – a rare and most welcome feature which could be encouraged. The preacher is not above contradiction. Sometimes it catches fire and I go out inspired.[4]

The practical manifestation of this shared but questioning journey appears in a number of ways: in the sermons preached; in the worshipping life of the church; in Lent Groups and other discussions; and in the Centre for Radical Christianity, with its conferences and 'Library Evenings', both of which frequently involve prestigious outside speakers.

Worship

St Mark's offers a variety of patterns of worship. On Sundays, the Book of Common Prayer is used at an 8.00am Eucharist, whilst less traditional liturgies, often drawing on patterns of worship from Taizé or Iona, are used in Night Service at 8.00pm. Not infrequently the latter is led by lay people rather than clergy. The main act of worship at 10.00am has also gradually moved away from traditional patterns and structures of worship to use forms of words that both are inclusive and also do not make impossible demands upon an individual's credulity. Whilst some parts of the liturgy may be drawn from the Church of England's *Common Worship*, other sources such as Taizé, Iona, the New Zealand Prayer book, the works of Jim Cotter and Janet Morley, or locally written texts, are used. These last are particularly important in giving voice to St Mark's theological understandings and thus offer readily understood meaning and relevance in congregational worship. Many are specially written for particular services. It used to be said of St Mark's that, if one walked around the church whilst the Nicene Creed was being said, one would undoubtedly hear the creed said in its entirety, but not everyone would feel able to say all of it. More accessible and appropriate liturgies mean that this story has become part of St Mark's folklore rather than being true of its current patterns of worship.

Music is an essential feature of worship at St Mark's and the church has been very fortunate in the organists it has been able to attract, its directors of music and the strength and depth of its choir. In addition to singing at the 10.00am service, the choir also perform at major festivals such as Advent and Passiontide. These special performances have utilised an expanded choir, drawing on the musical skills of many in the congregation who, for a variety of different reasons, are not normally part of the choir. Such participation enriches the sense of the community's involvement in worship.

Contributors to the 2010 Worship Survey noted the 'integrity and connectedness of the worship', the quality of the (lay led) intercessions and the quality of the music, including hymns, choir-led anthems and organ pieces. As one church member noted, 'at its best the 10.00am service pulls together and helps one to feel part of a greater, mysterious, unknowable yet fully knowable WHOLE'.[5] A similar comment could no doubt be made about (particularly) the 8.00pm service.

More especially, the integrity and connectedness reflected in the memorial services devised and developed after the (separate) tragic deaths of two widely known and much loved younger members of the congregation. In these examples, the liturgies arose directly from the experiences and feelings of those who had known the men concerned and in the case of one of them, who died from a brain tumour, had shared some of his last days with him.

Small groups

Small groups for prayer, contemplation or study remain an important part of church life for many. Some of these meet in the homes of participant members and operate independently of the church in general. Some involve members from other (non-Anglican) churches. The Lent study groups, however, are a long-standing feature of the church calendar, being used to encourage participants to reflect on selected theological or practical issues over a period of five weeks. Typically, they also involve members of sister churches in Broomhill and Broomhall. Recent topics have included the effects of climate change (and what might be done locally or nationally to address the issue) and the idea of 'paradise now'. Drawing on the book by Rita Brock and Rebecca Parker, *Saving Paradise*, and, in particular, utilising pictures of early religious mosaics from Ravenna in Italy, the course explored the first millennium understanding of paradise – that it is something to be experienced now rather than at some ill-defined time in the future. Such groups have proved to be a vital part of individual and (church) community development, offering individuals a safe opportunity to reconsider aspects of their faith and allow new understandings to emerge.

CRC and St Mark's Library Evenings

The Centre for Radical Christianity remains important as a focus for major conferences,

95. Tariq Ramadan, Professor of Contemporary Islamic Studies at the University of Oxford, addresses a conference of St Mark's Centre for Radical Christianity in May 2012.

attracting people from all parts of the UK. The conferences, with their attendant guest speakers, have helped shape the critical agenda of St Mark's; in recent years they have covered such diverse topics as 'Christa: the Female Christ' (Nicola Slee), 'Speaking Christian: Reclaiming Christian Language' (Marcus Borg) and 'Relating to the Other: A New Vision for Religious Pluralism' (Tariq Ramadan). They are complemented by periodic 'Library Evenings' at St Mark's, which frequently involve an invited author speaking about their book and the subject matter to which it relates. The library itself is, of course, a significant resource and offers a wide range of books of theological, biblical, liturgical, and socio-economic interest. It is particularly strong on writers whose theological approach has most influenced St Mark's in recent years such as Dominic Crossan and Marcus Borg, as well as holding material on contemporary issues such as interfaith dialogue and the reaction to the banking crisis of 2007-8.

Living Faith

We have a strong commitment to the inclusion of all. For example, we invite baptised children to take communion. We work within the structures of the Church of England to promote the inclusion of women in the episcopacy and the inclusion of gay, lesbian and bisexual Christians generally. Our main act of worship is welcoming, relevant and Anglican.

We consider matters of social justice to be central to the gospel. We are committed to supporting world development campaigns, climate change initiatives and to engaging with our community in alleviating the poverty on our doorstep. (Parish Profile, 2010)

Evidence of the congregation's living faith was clearly identified in a survey in 2011 that attempted to discover who was doing what within the congregation. An enormous number of

96. An inter-faith walk in Broomhall in November 2012.

activities were identified. Many of these were necessary maintenance tasks directed to ensuring that the church was open and available to those who might wish to use it. Many others fell into the 'social responsibility' category – caring in a variety of ways for those with particular needs. The list of these is almost endless and include the Lunch and Friendship Club (providing elderly members of the community with a weekly lunch and the opportunity to socialise); support for a worker with older people in conjunction with partner churches in Broomhill and Broomhall; the Soup Run – organised in conjunction with other churches in Sheffield – which takes soup and sandwiches once a week to people who are homeless or socially marginalised; and the weekly Broomhall Breakfast Club – run by St Mark's, St Andrew's and other local churches – which offers food and conversation to homeless people and anyone else who wishes to come.

Other activities in Broomhall include 'The Welcome Place', run jointly by St Mark's, the Broomhall Forum and the Broomhall Centre, which provides a place where people can be welcomed and local or personal issues can be aired. Experience has demonstrated that purposive activity that makes use of an individual's skills or helps develop new skills (sewing and cooking have been particularly successful) is an important part of building trust in this initiative.

The Broomhill Festival is also a significant reflection of a living faith. Although, strictly speaking, this is a local community venture rather than one run solely by St Mark's, a number of members of the congregation have played a very active part in ensuring its success over many years. It is an obvious illustration of the way in which the church is able to demonstrate what it can offer to the community by allowing its facilities to be used for concerts and other festival activities and by organising a Garden Party which attracts many to the church who would not otherwise make the opportunity to visit it.

In addition, a great deal of work is undertaken with younger people, both within St Mark's and outside it. For example, the CTBB (Churches Together in Broomhill and Broomhall) Youth Club for girls in Broomhall has been a success. One of its many benefits is the attempt to build linkages with a diverse ethnic community.

Many members of the church are also involved with matters of social concern outside the direct remit of the church – addressing the needs of asylum seekers, for example.

Environmental issues have concerned many members of the congregation, reflected not least in the Lent Series alluded to earlier and in the church's decision to seek recognition as an 'Eco Congregation'. The installation of photo-voltaic cells on the church roof in December 2011 was intended not only to benefit the church but also to be a visible demonstration of its commitment to the principles of carbon reduction. The substantial costs of the panels were comfortably met by donations from members of the congregation. A number of church members have formed a Carbon Reduction Action Group (CRAG) to provide group support for individuals' efforts to reduce their carbon emissions.

International concerns have always featured strongly at St Mark's, as earlier chapters have noted. However, the passage of time, together with changing international relationships, has resulted in the disappearance of links such as that established in the 1930s through the Church Missionary Society. More recent linkages with churches or projects overseas have also waned, although the congregation still has links with SUCCOL, which supports street children in Columbia. In addition, the International Fellowship established and active in the 1990s to welcome international students (in particular) to Broomhill has ceased to operate. Nevertheless, St Mark's remains committed to donating 10% of its given income to charities operating both overseas and in the UK, thus making a significant contribution to the work of a number of charities, many of them directly linked to the church through the activities of its members. There is active support for organisations such as Christian Aid, supplemented by 'bucket' collections to respond to sudden emergencies in developing countries.

Whilst many have expressed concern that St Mark's is good at thinking and poor at delivery, the activities outlined above offer a contrary view. Of course, not everyone can be engaged with them – nor do they need to be – and individuals' contributions may vary over time. Nonetheless, the activities highlighted above provide an illustration of a church committed to living the gospel in a variety of different ways. Moreover, constraints of space mean that this chapter has inevitably offered a less than comprehensive description of the variety of activities with which St Mark's is associated. Many of the concerns addressed by the congregation are not local but national. For example, many members have contributed to the campaign for women to be admitted to the episcopate. Similarly, many have been concerned about the Church of England's position on civil partnerships; at the time of writing, this position prohibits such partnerships being blessed in church. A very well attended open day in 2010 considered this issue, providing valuable support and encouragement to the PCC in its attempt to explore ways in which St Mark's might become a beacon of hope for those wishing to enter such a partnership in the context of their religious faith. The issue was especially salient because two well-loved and respected members of the congregation found themselves in just that position. Eventually a way forward was agreed which matched, with honesty and integrity, the radical tendencies of many in the congregation, the canon law of the Church of England and the wishes of the couple concerned. None of this was easy; inevitably the congregation does not speak with one voice. However, the process of discerning what was right was an important responsibility for the congregation and there was justifiable pleasure at the outcome achieved.

The Future

As always, the future will be a mixture of planned, intentional activity and responses to unforeseen issues. Many responses in the survey suggested that St Mark's should continue to be an example of what is possible when faith is *lived*. As one person put it: 'How far are we living out the kingdom values both as a community and within the community?' We will, of course, continue to try to further our understanding of 'kingdom values' through prayer, reflection and discussion. At the same time, our engagement with the challenge of living out kingdom values may take a variety of forms. Locally, the pressures on those parts of the parish most affected by social or economic deprivation continue to command the attention of the congregation. On a wider level, there is a need to engage with people of other faiths – not difficult to find in a multicultural city. National concerns, either within the church (helping promulgate the arguments for women bishops) or outside it (engaging with the economic, political and moral issues of the day), provide a continuing focus for our activities. The possibilities are endless. As one respondent to the 2012 survey noted:

As always, we should do everything. And God willing, He will help us … get somewhere with this enormous task.

Notes

[1] Minutes of St Mark's PCC, 12 February 2012.
[2] Parish Profile 2010.
[3] See also the *Results of the Worship Survey*, 2010.
[4] *Ibid.*, p. 9.
[5] *Ibid.*, p. 10.

CHAPTER 9

HOW TO READ ST MARK'S

Richard Taylor

As you approach St Mark's, the first thing you see is its spire (see Figure 57 on page 62). Victorian spires can be light, even playful – but not St Mark's. It speaks of an industrial city, of a time when goods from Sheffield were transported to every corner of a mighty Empire. It speaks of wealth – could the church have been built without money from those old industrialists? – but it is not showy, and it is certainly not frivolous. This was to be a working, functional building, and its spire would be solid and grave. Someone has attempted a decorative touch, with two small angels positioned half-way up the tower. But they look as if they have crept up from somewhere else, and are hoping that no one notices them. Even the church clock recalls the ubiquitous high street and factory clocks of the era, so vital for calling the hours of Victorian industry.

And then your eyes drift to the outside of the nave, and to the first surprise that St Mark's has to offer. Something dramatic happened here, and the pronounced pre- and post- War designs tell you that it was probably the War. From the outside, the windows of the new nave seem to be mixing it up a bit. They are regular, but playful, taking on different sizes and positions. The glass is clear, and you can see that the inside of the church must be filled with light. So you find yourself anticipating two distinct ways of sensing God's presence. The post-War nave recalls the churches of the Enlightenment, whose light-filled churches contained large windows of clear glass, as if to express the enlightened, rational nature of their faith. In contrast, the tower-end of St Mark's displays a Victorian sensibility, which favoured the mystery of faith, the flicker of candles, the glint of a chalice in the darkness. From the outside, the two ends of the church see-saw between different times, and different approaches to faith.

97. The winged lion, symbolising St Mark, created by the Revd Philip McFadyen, Curate 1971-74, and the young people (photograph: Richard Taylor).

St Mark is the second (many say the earliest) of the four gospel writers. Inside the entrance of the church is his symbol, a winged lion. The image is derived from visions of a mystical beast, seen by the prophet Ezekiel (Ezekiel 10 and 11) and in the Book of Revelation (4: 7-8). The beast had four faces, one of a man, one of bull, one of a lion and one of an eagle. Christian writers saw the beast with four faces as a symbol of the Gospel: four writers, but one Gospel. The face of the lion was said to symbolise Mark on the grounds that his gospel most concerns the kingship of Christ, and so should be symbolised by the king of the animals. The lion's open mouth and protruding tongue tell you that this is a speaking lion, telling out the Good News.

98. A Chapel window, designed by Gillian Rees-Thomas –'paths to heaven sway back and forth' (photograph: Richard Taylor).

As you enter the body of the church, to the right is the small side chapel, or Lady Chapel, where smaller services are held. At St Mark's, the chapel is austere – white-washed walls with touches of stone in the sanctuary, hard surfaces, a high ceiling. It is a space washed through with light, designed for prayer and quiet worship, monastic in its simplicity. It is easy to miss the beautiful abstract designs in the windows, by the artist Gillian Rees-Thomas. Vertical lines snake their way through the glass from bottom to top, cut across by horizontal lines. They call to mind the ladder on which angels ascended and descended between earth and heaven, which the patriarch Jacob saw in a dream (Genesis 28). As the ladders rise, they get narrower, and also more colourful, gradually filled with gorgeous browns, yellows, greys and little flashes of red. But the ladders sway and bend, and in some sections their steps turn sideways. If the design does indeed represent paths to and from God, then it was designed by someone who knew a little bit about faith.

Back in the main church, the font is set to the left of the nave. Above it is a round of girders, a feature designed to separate and denote the baptism space as sacred, special. At baptism, heaven and earth in some sense touch, and in many churches the site of the font is decorated with flowers, flames or stars. At St Mark's, the metalwork acts as a crown, while the font-cover looks like fire.

Step back into the nave and ahead of you is St Mark's most potent set of symbols – the great east window, designed by Henry Stammers. The glass is set between the branches of a tree, which shoot right and left from a trunk that rises to the right of the altar. Is this the tree of life?

The glass itself sees the world gathered in wonder and worship of the Trinity. At the very top, a hand descends from the clouds, representing God the Father. This is a '*Manus Dei*' (Hand of God), an ancient symbol of God. When two fingers of the hand are extended, as here, it indicates God's blessing.

Below is the central image, of God the Son, Jesus Christ. Christ is dressed as king and priest. He is wearing a king's crown, and is dressed in priest's robes, a chasuble that seems to be decorated with a blood-red cross, and tassels of a stole peeping out below. He is a young Christ, shown clean shaven, reminiscent of the very earliest representations of Jesus in Greek art (he only took on a beard in the eleventh century). Jesus is shown in a crucifixion pose, with arms outstretched, but is not crucified. This is Christ triumphant, shown not in agony on the cross, but having completed his sacrifice and opening his arms for all. The cross itself retreats into the background, although just below the hand of God you see the letters '*INRI*', for *Iesus Nazarenus Rex Iudaeorum*, 'Jesus of Nazareth, King of the Jews', the words that Pontius Pilate ordered to be nailed to Christ's cross.

The image of Christ triumphant is in sharp contrast to the cross that stands behind the altar. This cross speaks of pitiless violence. Long iron nails savagely cut through its hands and feet. The statue is made from girders, like the crown above the font, and like those manufactured all over South Yorkshire. The contemporary local materials suggest that the violence and sacrifice of the

99: East end, with organ casing, 'Te Deum' window by Henry Stammers and pulpit
(photographs: Richard Taylor).

99A: St Joan of Arc.

99B Mary Magdalene, carrying a jar
of spices to anoint Christ's body,
hears from an angel that he is risen.

99C Working class, middle
class, upper class –
everyone condemns Jesus.

99D A grasshopper and a mouse,
on Easter morning.

crucifixion is not a distant event, but is here, and now.

Returning to the east window, below the image of Jesus is an image of the Holy Spirit, the third person of the Trinity, in the traditional form of a dove. The image comes from the baptism of Christ, when the spirit of God is said to have descended on Christ in this form. Here, the dove has a cruciform halo (a halo run through with a cross), which is the form of halo used by artists to honour Christ. The fact that the Holy Spirit is given a cruciform halo, like Jesus, is another allusion to the Trinity. It is a statement that Christ and the Holy Spirit are of one being.

The multitude gazing at the Trinity consists of angels (hovering high above, some of them in pretty uncomfortable positions), crowned kings, turbaned sultans and ordinary men and women. All beings – spiritual and physical, alive and dead, of all nations and of every social status – are gathered to adore God. In one light, a medieval Crusader stands in a pointed helmet with his Cross-of-St-George shield, while in front of him a modern man in sunglasses cranes his neck upwards.

Three individuals are identifiable, all of them in the bottom row. At the far left is St Catherine, standing beside her burning wheel. St Catherine had a brilliant intellect, and the Emperor Maximinius challenged her to debate the claims of Christ with 50 male philosophers. Catherine trounced the lot of them and, for her success, was condemned to death on a burning wheel (hence the name of the spinning firework, the Catherine Wheel). Slightly to the right of the dove of the Holy Spirit is an image of St John the Baptist, dressed in his wild, camel-hair clothes and carrying a long thin cross. St John is one of the patron saints of pilgrimage, and is often shown carrying this lightweight pilgrim's cross. In his hand is a scallop shell, another symbol of pilgrimage (pilgrims used the shells as shallow scoops for drinking water from the streams they passed). Further to the right of St John is Joan of Arc, dressed in armour and carrying a battle flag. So we have an intellectual, a wild man and a warrior – very St Mark's.

The great architectural critic Nikolai Pevsner did not go for the east window of St Mark's at all. He described it as 'wild', and there is a case to be made that the artist worked better on a smaller scale, in the set of windows behind the altar. The images here are delightful, with the feel of a child's storybook. They tell the story of Christ in four panels: from the left, the Annunciation and Nativity, the Passion, the Resurrection, and the Ascension. The artistic language that the windows adopt is derived from the Middle Ages; the effect is like watching a cycle of medieval mystery plays.

The Annunciation and Nativity are to the left, outside the sanctuary. The Angel Gabriel announces the coming of Christ to Mary; angels announce his birth to shepherds; and kings visit the new-born Christ. The Angel Gabriel is dressed in medieval style, with feathers. Feathers would have been used in angel costumes in the mystery plays, and medieval images of angels tend to be feathered too (the Victorians preferred their angels in floaty gowns; the Georgians, chubby cherubs). The next panel in the series, at the left of the sanctuary, shows Christ crucified, mourned helplessly by his mother, Mary, and companions John and Mary Magdalene. The artist has included a meditational favourite from the Middle Ages, the 'Instruments of the Passion'. These are isolated articles from the Passion, separated out so that the prayerful can meditate on them one by one. So, you find the crown of thorns, the cross, the nails, the hammer used to drive them home, the spear that stuck in Christ's side, pliers used to extract the nails, and so on. There are modern touches, too. The mocking of Christ is shown by a man spitting, who is doffing three different hats, one of them an upper-class top-hat, one a middle-class bowler hat and one a labourer's cap. The image tells us that Christ was condemned by men from every station of life. The third panel, to the right behind the altar, shows the Resurrection – or rather, the announcement of the Resurrection by an angel (still in feathers!) at the entrance to the empty tomb. Behind the angel stands Golgotha, with its three, now empty, crosses. One of these windows, tucked behind the altar, is my own favourite. It shows the simple beauty of nature on that spring Easter morning, with vines, flowers, even a little grasshopper. The fourth and final panel, to the far right, shows the Ascension. Again, the image is medieval. Christ's feet disappear into the clouds (in the mystery plays the actor playing Christ, or a model of Christ, may have been winched heavenwards) leaving their imprint on the stone below, while the disciples look upwards in wonder.

To the left of the east window is the organ casing, a fine piece of design, which it is easy to overlook. A lazy solution to covering the organ pipes would have been to erect a plain grid. Instead, with a series of simple tweaks, the designer has terminated the grids at different levels, pulled some part of them outwards, and introduced irregularity among the rectangles. The effect is architectural, and makes the casing look like an abstract sculpture of a vast, pure-white city. Is this a heavenly Jerusalem?

Across from the organ is the most solid pulpit that you will ever see. Built of closely-fitted stones in identical rectangles, it gives the impression of a harbour wall, or impregnable fortress. The heavy, block-y solidity makes it feel like an immoveable rock of ages, and if you look closely at the stone you will find that it is riddled with tiny fossils, millions of years old. These are ancient stones from which to proclaim the unending Word of God.

Above the pulpit is one of St Mark's most dramatic and unique features. Many pulpits include a 'sounding board', a flat structure over the preacher's head that helps to project the sound of the preacher's voice to the congregation. Sounding boards are a feature of English pulpits, particularly from the eighteenth century, when preaching was a central feature of the church service. The structure above the pulpit at St Mark's is a brilliant reference to these old boards. It is huge, sweeping dramatically into the air. It is not used to amplify the speaker so much as to focus attention on him or her in a visual way, while hopefully encouraging his or her words to soar.

But St Mark's saves the best for last. As you leave the church, you see at the rear its most famous artwork, a stained-glass window from the hand of the great English designer, John Piper. On the day of Pentecost, when the Holy Spirit visited the disciples, tongues of fire appeared and touched each one of them (Acts 2). Piper's image is of the fire of the Holy Spirit, darting, soaring and blazing in reds, yellows and oranges.

But here is a question: is the fire shooting downwards, or jumping upwards? Each tongue has a small head, with a tail of fire trailing behind it. Some seem to be descending from heaven towards the congregation; others are leaping upwards, as if the congregation is firing back! The effect is thrilling, a joyful dance, and a reminder to people as they leave the church that they have the power to light up the world.

100. The west window, showing the Holy Spirit, designed by John Piper and executed by Patrick Reyntiens. Dedicated by the Bishop of Sheffield in December 1963 (photograph: Philip Wright).

CHAPTER 10

CLOSING REFLECTIONS

Ian Wallis

As sitting incumbent at the time when this volume was in preparation, it is my good fortune to be able to contribute directly, not by way of an account of the most recent years (that task rightly falls to another), but in the form of closing reflections in which I shall attempt to highlight some of the continuities and developments, formative influences and defining characteristics of St Mark's emerging from previous chapters. I have made no attempt to be systematic or comprehensive and inevitably what is written reflects my own perspective, but hopefully these comments will go some way towards gathering together an answer to Professor Marcus Borg's question posed at the outset, 'I wonder how long it takes to grow a congregation like St Mark's?'

A Parish Church

One of the gifts of the established church to the nation has been an enduring commitment to maintaining a parochial system and, with it, a Christian presence throughout the land, enabling ministry in Christ's name to be offered, in most cases without cost, to all parishioners, irrespective of their church-going proclivities. Throughout a history that has accommodated significant boundary changes, successive incumbents of St Mark's and, since their inception, PCCs have sought to fulfil this vocation, as is demonstrated by investments in capital projects (e.g., Ashgate Road Rooms, Broomhall Mission Hall, Coldwell Lane Sports Field), additional personnel (e.g., assistant clergy, lay workers) and outreach initiatives (e.g., uniformed organisations, community groups, ecumenical projects, Broomhill Festival). What is more, it appears that, at least in the early decades, most of the congregation resided within the parish and many parishioners looked to St Mark's for baptisms, marriages and funerals. Yet, even in the days of the iron church, Criticus (a Victorian precursor, by the sounds of it, to the 'mystery worshipper' of the current *Ship of Fools* website!) was commenting on the rarefied and refined climate of St Mark's – reflecting, no doubt, the composition of the congregation. With time, the balance between worshippers residing within or beyond the parish boundary would swing in favour of the latter, suggesting a loosening of associational connections between the church and its parishioners.

Reasons for this are not difficult to identify: for one thing, the lack of parochial coherence and definition. Arbitrary is an apt word for the parish boundaries in their various iterations, embracing areas with little in common, separated by delimiters such as major public highways, and with no obvious centre to which parish residents would be drawn. What is more, once the decision was taken to build the first stone church set back from Glossop Road, St Mark's has gradually become less visible to the community, to the extent that it is now masked by trees to the south, overshadowed by the Royal Hallamshire Hospital and its halls of residence to the east and north, and hidden behind the Rutland Hotel to the west. Another factor relates to accessibility. Gaining entrance to the new church is far from straightforward, especially if you are approaching from Glossop Road. There is also the possibility that incumbents and congregations have given rise to expressions of Christianity that parishioners have not readily related to or wished to make their own. Another consideration is the rise of secularism, especially during the second half of the twentieth century and within communities open to Enlightenment thinking.

A Gathered Congregation

From the outset, St Mark's has attracted sizeable congregations who have appreciated a particular flavour of Anglicanism, and who have, more often than not, been well-resourced both intellectually and financially. Equally, they have had high expectations and standards, yielding members who have wished to become actively involved in the shaping of church policy as well as in its execution. And whilst, as we have seen, the flavour has not remained constant – with regard to changes in theological perspective, for example – allegiance has endured.

One consequence of such an ecclesial community has been the emergence of a church with a vision extending beyond parochial borders, readily engaging in the social, political and economic challenges of the day, as well as seeking to respond to humanitarian concerns, globally as much as locally. Another has been a readiness to participate in the life of the broader church, whether in terms of finance, faithfully paying its 'share' as well as raising funds for special diocesan projects, or through members being willing to serve at deanery, diocesan or General Synod levels. Equally, a wider perspective has engendered a capacity for entertaining fresh ideas and influences within the life of St Mark's – liturgically, theologically and architecturally.

If the current incarnation is any guide, then one of the essential ingredients of congregations at St Mark's is friendship. Not simply acquaintance or friendliness, but fruitful friendships extending beyond church life and continuing long after individuals move away. Friendships are able to bring stability to church life, especially in times of hardship or transition, and provide a natural network of pastoral care. Friendships build allegiance, as well as a willingness to participate fully in church life and take on fresh challenges. There are great strengths in such togetherness, so long as friendship is exercised with a mindfulness of newcomers as well as of others who do not yet belong to a 'community within the community'.

Architectural Innovation

As previous chapters have chronicled, winning the argument for the rebuilding of St Mark's after it was gutted by fire and then mustering the wherewithal to bring it about proved to be a herculean task that, without the passionate tenacity of incumbents Gleave and Adie, together with a small team of equally outstanding lay persons, would almost certainly have failed. The conservative option would have been to replicate the Victorian church; the appointment of George Pace as architect, however, signalled the onset of change – a decision, as the ensuing years have demonstrated, with implications reaching far beyond the creation of a remarkable worship space. While integrating parts of its predecessor, the new St Mark's, with its uncluttered interior and angular asymmetry, its lofty perpendiculars and resplendent spaciousness, its accessible sanctuary and broad communion table presided over by the risen Christ, speaks of a hospitable faith emerging from (but unencumbered by) the past, enlightened by its founder, open to the world, comfortable with innovation. If the exterior gives little away and gaining access can be a bit of a struggle, once inside there is ample space to be – to gain fresh perspective and contemplate one's place within a momentum of faith reaching back to first-century Galilee. In many respects, the new St Mark's invites, even expects, an exploratory, pioneering approach to Christianity. It is a building that fosters a very particular vocation.

Theological Pioneering

One of the dangers of a history project such as this (hopefully, averted in this case!) is that it conveys an impression of church life as a theatrical performance of many acts, in which successive incumbents and their colleagues perform on stage to the appreciation, bewilderment or disapproval of their audiences. Yet, as a worshipper from a former parish insisted at the end of my first service,

'Remember, you're the one who's passing through.' It was hard to hear, but apt. The church *is* its members, with the principal source of embodiment and continuity supplied by the congregation rather than by the clergy. What is more, churches tend to be at their most fruitful when there is resonance and reciprocity between incumbent and congregation, where the former is not trying to impose and members of the latter are able to influence. Such a climate engenders creativity and flourishing whilst freeing up time and energy to look outwards and to participate in the broader mission of Christ.

Through its history there has been a significant movement in theological perception at St Mark's, from a faith characterised by Protestant evangelicalism, so prevalent in Sheffield throughout the nineteenth century, to one informed by progressive liberalism, heralded by the publication of *Honest to God* by Bishop John Robinson in the same year as the new church was consecrated. By any measure, this was a major transition, coincidental with and to some measure, no doubt, precipitated by the new building. If evolution through organic growth – with intelligent, outward-looking clergy and laity collaborating in what it means to be true to the gospel – describes the life of St Mark's up to this point, then something radically different happened in the 1960s – something that, for the faithful remnant who had continued to worship in St Mark's Hall on Ashgate Road, must have had more than a whiff of revolution about it.

In the light of its pedigree, the appointment of a young liberal catholic to the incumbency of St Mark's was a gamble. Michael Adie had been invited to apply by Leslie Hunter, then Bishop of Sheffield, but he was of a different theological outlook and liturgical style from his predecessors. According to Adie, the bishop's recommendation owed more to his strategy for student mission in the area than to any intention to steer St Mark's in a different direction. But the latter occurred as a consequence, and must surely have been anticipated by Hunter. In truth, though, it was opportune, with a confluence of factors giving rise to a fresh embodiment of faith – a gifted priest eager to make the most of a new building set in university heartland, during an unprecedented period of liturgical experimentation within the Church of England and a zeitgeist of permissiveness and improvisation that permeated at least certain quarters of Sheffield. This was, indeed, a radical departure – a kind of resurrection born out of an equally radical destruction. Adie's impact upon St Mark's was substantial, with an enduring legacy still appreciated today. One wonders what his contribution within the Diocese more broadly would have been had synergies with Hunter's successor been stronger.

Evolution and organic growth soon returned within a new climate as a revived and vibrant congregation began to gather, unfamiliar with former incarnations of St Mark's, open to new learning and with an increasing confidence and capacity for shaping its future. During the ensuing years, aided by developments in New Testament scholarship, the witness and ministry of Jesus of Nazareth increasingly came into focus as the source of Christian faith and inspiration for contemporary discipleship. One expression of this new momentum is the Centre for Radical Christianity, fruit of Adrian Alker's years, which champions progressive approaches to faith rooted in Jesus and is committed to rigorous intellectual engagement with other disciplines of human inquiry, as well as with the challenges facing humanity at large. CRC not only gives expression to St Mark's current passions and commitments, but also invites others of similar outlook around the UK to meet, gain fresh insight and find encouragement among kindred spirits.

Liturgical Creativity

As you would expect within a church attracting members from beyond the parish, the style and quality of worship have been defining, and greatly valued, components of St Mark's throughout, consistently drawing comment from members of the congregation whilst requiring careful consultation by incumbents before change is implemented. From the beginning, there appears to have been an intolerance of fussiness or excessive ceremonialism, with the stress firmly upon the fundamentals, which interestingly extended beyond word and sacrament to include music and a choir. Liturgical revisions within the Church of England have been embraced with varying degrees of enthusiasm and, whilst recent decades have witnessed greater experimentation, drawing on sources beyond those authorised by Canon Law, most main services have remained identifiably Anglican in structure and spirit. This is particularly noteworthy in the light of the major shift in theological perspective mentioned above, which could have resulted in liturgical worship being deemed prescriptive or overly constraining, as has happened elsewhere in the Church of England.

So far, this has not been the case. In fact, the form of the Eucharistic rite remains a valued component of the main act of Sunday worship – providing stability, continuity and direction, as well as a framework capable of being fleshed out with different compositions of words to express seasonal emphases or theological conviction. It also exerts a measured discipline, a friendly constraint, within an environment of creativity and exploration.

Liberal progressiveness, however, has spawned new opportunities for worship to supplement existing ones. Services have developed that are more able to accommodate those unfamiliar with or no longer able to relate to traditional formulations – experimental, contemplative and non-dogmatic in approach, incorporating silence and innovative ways of relating to the sacred. In one sense, this can be seen as simply the latest expression of a long-standing commitment to offering accessible worship, which has also spawned family and all-age services as well as home-grown nativity plays. Yet, in another, it represents a growing confidence in newly discovered ways of conceiving faith and concomitant urgency for such faith to find liturgical form and expression.

Although it is difficult to generalise, one component of worship consistently valued through time has been what can be described as intelligent preaching with an emphasis upon the substance of the message rather than the performance of the preacher – although the pulpits of St Mark's have held many fine orators – with sermons able to reach beyond the horizon of the Biblical text and theological discourse to bring into focus the issues and challenges of responsible Christian living in a world of injustice and need; sermons informed by and engaging with the learning of other disciplines of human inquiry, open to insights from beyond the teaching of the church.

Inclusive Hospitality

If it were possible to transport someone from the early years of St Mark's into the present day, I wonder what he or she would comment on? The architecture, certainly, but also, I suspect, the attire of worshippers, the diverse, cosmopolitan composition of the congregation and an atmosphere of relaxed informality capable of embracing people of differing background, outlook and opinion. And what about the centrality of the Eucharist, women priests, civil partnerships, liturgical variety and experimentation, greater lay participation, children receiving the sacrament, amplification and hearing loops, toilets and a kitchen, refreshments and Sunday lunch, not to overlook Churches Together in Broomhill and Broomhall, ecumenism and a programme of social action and humanitarian relief?

One hopes there would be areas of familiarity and continuity as well, but the overriding sense would be one of change and, with that, at least a measure of strangeness. And whilst components within this process of evolution have been precipitated by various factors, taken together they can be seen as cairns on a journey towards inclusive hospitality, with more and more people being invited, encouraged and enabled to receive the good news of the kingdom and to respond in a way that resonates with them personally. Significantly, though, for all that the current landscape would appear unfamiliar, it is a journey whose start can be traced back to the days of the iron church when pew rents were in force. At a time when the discriminatory nature of this means of financing church life was only beginning to be recognised, it is perhaps encouraging to learn that the free pews for the poor within the first St Mark's were furnished to the same standard as those rented out. Where this journey into inclusive hospitality will lead in the future is probably as difficult for us to anticipate as it would have been for our Victorian forebears to envisage the St Mark's of 2013.

A Political Faith

Judging from the findings of previous chapters, St Mark's has rarely, if ever, been a place where politics and religion were considered unrelated or intentionally kept apart. On the contrary, the political implications of the gospel reverberate through its 150-year history, albeit interpreted in strikingly different ways, but with commonalities in the agenda to be addressed, notably humanitarian concerns for our neighbours locally, nationally and internationally. Although the current congregation of St Mark's is far from homogenous in terms of party political allegiance, it bears witness to a movement away from conservative, establishment values of former times (cf. Canon Gleave's comments on the Cold War referred to in chapter 4) to embrace a more radical agenda that seeks not only to respond charitably to those in need, but also to challenge systemic injustice and oppressive regimes that reinforce social inequality and oppression. Allied to this, is a commitment to working towards a society rooted in Jesus' kingdom values, and yielding a sustainable economy characterised by responsible environmental stewardship, welfare provision for the vulnerable and a fairer distribution of wealth – a commitment finding expression in political activism and a prophetic voice, as well as in humanitarian aid and service.

Active Compassion

St Mark's has been fortunate through its years to attract well-resourced congregations. Reassuringly, this has fostered a responsible and generous attitude towards giving, especially when focused on those in greatest need, whether in the parish or beyond. The provision of amenities on Ashgate Road, Broomspring Lane and Coldwell Lane previously mentioned are early examples of responding locally, and represent substantial financial investment. Whilst congregations of the new church have not undertaken comparable capital projects (although the kitchen and lounge extension have benefitted the community), the commitment to serving vulnerable and disadvantaged members in the locality has remained resolute, as evidenced by initiatives such as Broomhall Breakfast Club, Credit Union outlet, Drop-ins and Youth Clubs, plus the Eldon Street 'Soup Wagon', St Mark's Lunch and Friendship Club, and the employment of assistant staff with community development experience or expertise in working with older people.

This pronounced sense of social responsibility, however, has never been a simply parochial affair. In addition to supporting ministry in less prosperous parts of the diocese through the parish share system of allocating the diocesan budget according to means, and capital injections to fund particular initiatives (e.g., rebuilding of St Bartholomew's), there has consistently been a willingness to engage regionally, nationally and globally in programmes of humanitarian relief and regeneration. Over the years, this has fostered long and lasting relationships with established charities (e.g., Christian Aid and USPG) and given rise to new ones, with members becoming personally involved (e.g., 'Literacy for Life' in Ghana, 'Sakhelwe' in South Africa and 'SUCCOL' in Columbia). Thankfully, this spirit of active compassion continues unabated through the current climate of fiscal austerity – a recent 'one-off' appeal following a Sunday service for which no prior notice had been given raised nearly £2,000, there and then.

Confident (Un)Believing

Leafing through earlier editions of *The Messenger*, I was struck by the fact that St Mark's used to sponsor an overseas missionary – something that wealthy evangelical churches continue to do. It is difficult to envisage today's congregation undertaking such an initiative. During the second half of the twentieth century, our understanding of mission and evangelism, as with humanitarian aid, has developed, and with that has come a greater appreciation of God's ubiquitous providence, as well as of the importance of respecting difference and encouraging self-determination. What is significant, however, is that, whilst St Mark's would no longer describe itself as evangelical in terms of churchmanship and theology, it nevertheless remains passionate about the good news of Jesus Christ and enthusiastic about sharing it with others in ways that are true to the gospel – causing one recent Church Army trainee serving a placement at St Mark's to contemplate the 'unlikely notion of liberal evangelism'.

To date, St Mark's has managed to avoid one of the cardinal sins besetting liberal churches, namely becoming so preoccupied with what is no longer believable in Christianity that faith is all but emptied of meaning, vitality and hope. No doubt, the gospel of St Mark's today would be expressed in different language and give rise to different responses from those espoused by earlier congregations, but it would be no less rooted in the founder of Christian faith nor less compelling in its contemporary relevance. It would seek to make the Galilean visible once more, unencumbered by doctrinal interpretation or credal formulation, so that the authority of his humanity shines through – his wisdom and vision, his passion for justice and truth, his energising being-in-relation to God, his capacity for healing, forgiveness and loving, his commitment to the marginalised and downtrodden, his genius for creating community and extending hospitality to the wayward and ostracised, his grounding of spirituality within the earthiness of existence, his ability to affirm life and engender a fuller, profounder quality of human being in others: a 'this-worldly' Jesus with a message and way of life for here and now, one content to entrust the future into God's hands.

A Lion with Eagle's Wings

An interesting piece of information to emerge from this history project is that St Mark's was almost dedicated to St John. Reassuringly, we were wedded to the lion! I suspect that, for all his or her profundity, the lofty theologizing and other-worldliness of the fourth evangelist would have made for awkward company over the years. For all our intellectual endeavour, we are better suited to the second, whose gospel of action bears witness to a Jesus who spends relatively little time talking about the Kingdom of God and invests most of his energies in bringing it about – realising the transformative potential of God's justice, forgiveness, wisdom and grace. In Mark's Gospel, Jesus is the archetypal practitioner of faith – liberating the oppressed, ministering to the needy, confronting evil, challenging corruption and the misuse of power. Yet he does not work alone, and recruited apprentices from the outset. And as the disciples watch and learn, they come to recognise the universal reach of God's loving purposes and the costly demands of being channels for its realisation. Then, after the crucifixion, they are enjoined to return to Galilee, where Jesus will be encountered once more.

There are no resurrection narratives in the second Gospel, only an invitation to discover the risen Christ in his service – gathering in his name, following his example, daring to believe that what he lived and died for demands our best endeavour and last breath. It is to this vocation that St Mark's seeks to bear witness.

APPENDIX 1

CLERGY AND CHURCH WARDENS

VICARS

Note: From 1867 to 1871, the Revd William Milton was Minister to the iron church, which served the ecclesiastical district of St Mark's Broomhall. With the consecration of the stone church on 31 May 1871, he became Vicar of the parish of St Mark's Broomhall. In 1991, the title of the parish was changed to St Mark's Broomhill.

1867-71	The Revd William Milton – Minister, District of St Mark's Broomhall
1871-84	The Revd William Milton – Vicar, St Mark's Broomhall
1884-96	The Ven. Henry Arnold Favell, Archdeacon of Sheffield
1896-1905	The Revd Alfred Pearson
1905-11	The Rt Revd Dr John Nathaniel Quirk, Bishop of Sheffield
1911-21	The Revd Arthur Burnet Burney
1921-31	The Revd Ernest Mannering
1931-59	The Revd John Wallace Gleave (later Canon Gleave)
1960-69	The Revd Michael Adie
1969-78	The Revd Michael Paton
1978-87	The Revd John Giles
1988-2008	The Revd Adrian Alker (from 2005, Canon Alker)
2009-	The Revd Dr Ian Wallis

CURATES AND OTHER CLERGY

Note: This list includes only those clergy holding a specific office at St Mark's, so university and hospital chaplains, retired clergy, etc. have not been included. Comprehensive information about curates between 1871 and 1919 is not available. The list of curates below has therefore been compiled from Baptism Registers, Registers of Services and press reports. The dates when they were at St Mark's are in some cases approximate.

1870-72	Curate	The Revd Benjamin Hunter
1873-75	Curate	The Revd C. Unwin
1875-77	Curate	The Revd T.J. Rawson
1878-84	Curate	The Revd W.M. Tomlinson
1884-88	Curate	The Revd P Houghton
1888-1900	Curate	The Revd T.C. Davies
1895-97	Curate	The Revd N. Storrs Fox
1899-1900	Curate	The Revd D Davies
1900-1	Curate	The Revd Sydney Smith
1901-3	Curate	The Revd A.C. Macmill
1901-7	Curate	The Revd C.G. Lane
1903-5	Curate	The Revd J. Haythornthwaite
1905-7	Curate	The Revd John Young

1907-11	Curate	The Revd C.H. Moxley
1907-10	Curate	The Revd John Bentley
1909-11	Curate	The Revd M. Young
1911-13	Curate	The Revd J.E. Lamin
1911-15	Curate	The Revd Reginald Bentley
1914-18	Curate	The Revd C.W.B. Haslam
1918-19	Curate	The Revd H. Wood
1919-20	Curate	The Revd J. Garfield Roberts
1921-24	Curate	The Revd J.W. Gleave
1927-32	Curate	The Revd D. Hopkins
1932-38	Curate	The Revd A. King
1939-41	Curate	The Revd A.B. Swallow
1953-57	Curate	The Revd G. Neville
1961-65	Curate	The Revd Edward Longman
1965-68	Curate	The Revd David Ellington
1968-70	Curate	The Revd Andrew Butcher
1971-74	Curate	The Revd Philip McFadyen
1975-78	Curate	The Revd David Gay
1991-95	Curate	The Revd Dr Jane Tillier
1995-97	Curate	The Revd Hilary Jowett
1997-2000	Curate	The Revd Jane Bolton
2000-2	Assoc. Vicar	The Revd Jane Bolton
2002-4	Assoc. Vicar	The Revd Sally Fairweather
2005-9	Asst Priest	The Revd Sue Hobley
2010-	Assoc. Vicar	The Revd Sue Hammersley
2010-	Curate	The Revd Shan Rush

CHURCH WARDENS

1869	Henry Rodgers, John Edward Cutler
1873	Theophilus Marsh, H. Clifton Sorby
1878	David Ward, Francis Hobson
1885	David Ward, C.E. Vickers
1888	C.E. Vickers, J. Hunt
1889	J. Hunt, K. Kingsford Wilson
1890	J Kingsford Wilson, B. Burdekin
1891	B. Burdekin, C.D. Pettinger
1892	C.D. Pettinger, H.P. Marsh
1896	C.D. Pettinger, C.F. Longden
1898	C.D. Pettinger, J.D. Webster
1899	Geo. Williams, J.D. Webster
1901	Geo. Williams, H.P. Burdekin
1902	H.P. Marsh, H.P. Burdekin
1903	H.P. Marsh, S. Richardson
1904	H.M. Benson, H. Green
1906	H. Green, J. Henderson
1908	H.B. Sandford, J. Henderson
1910	N.W. Burbridge, J. Henderson
1911	N.W. Burbridge, S. Gardner Harrison
1912	E.C. Benson, S. Gardner Harrison

1913	E.C. Benson, B.H. Hoole
1914	B.H. Hoole, N.W. Burbridge
1915	O.H. Lace, B.H. Hoole
1916	C.J. Collier, W.E. Gray
1918	J. Douglas Webster, S. Hallam
1919	J. Douglas Webster, Sholto Douglas
1920	J. Douglas Webster, H. Michael Elliott
1922	Lawrence Jackson, H. Michael Elliott
1923	Lawrence Jackson, A.M. Baily
1924	H. Michael Elliott, Bernard H. Hoole
1928	H. Michael Elliott, Edgar C. Benson
1934	B.W. Watson, J.W. Boddy
1939	B.W. Watson, Rowland H. Williams
1942	J.W. Boddy, Rowland H. Williams
1943	Percy T. Barnsley, Rowland H. Williams
1951	William H. Wilcockson, Rowland H. Williams
1955	William Wilcockson, Ernest A. Hayes
1964	Ernest Hayes, Lt Col. George Field
1965	Lt Col. George Field, Ray Holehouse
1968	Ray Holehouse, Roy Godden
1971	John E. Johnson, Roy Godden
1973	Leslie Fillmore, Roy Godden
1974	Leslie Fillmore, Emlyn Perrett
1976	Emlyn Perrett, Ken Jones
1978	Ken Jones, Tony Rogers
1980	Tony Rogers, Prof. David McClean
1981	Prof. David McClean, Robin Saunders
1984	Robin Saunders, Margaret Lyons
1985	Margaret Lyons, Julian Garland
1986	Margaret Lyons, Chris Knight
1988	Chris Knight, Jennifer Powell
1990	Jennifer Powell, David Ryder
1992	David Ryder, Judith Pitchforth
1994	David Ryder, Jane Padget
1995	Jane Padget, Tim Hill
1996	Tim Hill, BrionyTayler
1999	Briony Tayler, David Price
2001	Louise White, David Price
2002	David Price, Kay Hudson
2003	Kay Hudson, Keith Pitchforth
2006	Keith Pitchforth, Jane Padget
2007	Jane Padget, Martin Godley
2010	Jane Padget, Gary Grief
2011	Gary Grief, Michael Hunt

APPENDIX 2

STATISTICS OF COMMUNICANTS, ATTENDANCE AND ELECTORAL ROLL

YEAR	NORMAL SUNDAY COMMUNICANTS OCT AVERAGE	AVERAGE SUNDAY ATTENDANCE IN OCTOBER	ELECTORAL ROLL (Brackets indicate number not residing in parish)
1960	23		258
1961	35		258
1962	67		
1963	115		242
1964	149		
1965	157		
1966	165		
1967	158		
1968	146	205	
1969	150		
1970	136		
1971	166		257
1972	159		218
1973	151		230
1974	143		235
1975	134		233
1976	142		221
1977	138		
1978	170	215	
1979	191		
1980	161		
1981	191		
1982	182		
1983	173		
1984	168		
1985	167		
1986	140		
1987	130		199
1988	135		192
1989	145		228
1990	141	231	179
1991	140	225	195
1992	150	228	208
1993	150	212	215
1994	135	202	200

1995	154	193	189
1996	172	220	181
1997	136	193	187 (124)
1998	132	222	184
1999	160	171	184
2000	155	178	197 (130)
2001	188	203	201
2002	197	225	155 (95)
2003	195	226	202 (136)
2004	170	209	216 (149)
2005	169	197	230 (160)
2006	143	160	249 (174)
2007	177	195	213 (161)
2008	154	174	233 (177)
2009	162	177	233 (177)
2010	142	161	231 (175)
2011	177	194	214 (156)
2012	180	197	215 (159)

NOTES

1. These figures have been obtained from the Archbishops' Council statistician, Registers of Services, reports at Annual Meetings or at the PCC and current church officers. Interpretation and methods of collection will have varied over 50 years.

2. **Electoral rolls.** Our information from before 1987 is incomplete. The electoral roll is anyway an inadequate indicator of congregational size, because numbers build up over the six-year cycle between complete revisions and then reduce again when a new roll is produced.

3. **Average October Sunday communicants.** Average numbers for October communicants are a better indicator of church attendance. Communicant numbers were boosted by the introduction of Parish Communion in 1961 and the opening of the new church building in September 1963. The figures then fluctuate generally between 130 and 180, though following the admission of children to Communion in November 2000, the numbers exceeded 180 for the next three years. For the significance of these figures, see comments by the Revd Michael Paton, Vicar 1970-78, on page 82.

4. **Average Sunday attendance.** The average Sunday attendance figure has been recorded since 1990 and gives the most comprehensive picture. It is the main basis for the Church of England's current 'Statistics for Mission'. By chance, the Register of Services does give us these data for 1968 and 1978.

5. Information on weekday communicants is not included, as numbers are small compared with Sunday.

6. Similarly, occasional offices have not been included as their numbers are relatively low at St Mark's; e.g., in 2001, there were 11 baptisms, 4 marriages, and 3 funerals in church and 14 funerals at the crematorium or cemetery.

APPENDIX 3

The Stained Glass in St Mark's Stone Church

In May to September 1940, *St Mark's Parish Magazine* published a series of articles describing the stained glass in the Church. This was extraordinarily timely, since all the glass was to be blown to smithereens in December of that year. We lack any close up pictures of these windows, but we do have the descriptions, from which the following summaries and quotations are taken.

The East Window

This was the large window above the altar, facing the congregation. It was dedicated: 'To the glory of God, and in memory of Samuel Parker, of Broomgrove, who died 30th December 1871, aged 83. Erected by Jane, his daughter, and her husband, Theophilus Marsh'.

The upper, larger window showed 'the Ascension of our Lord as He is watched by wondering disciples and friends' with the text: 'While He blessed them He was parted from them, and carried up into Heaven'. The lower left hand panel depicted 'the Burial of our Lord, illustrating the text: "He made His grave with the wicked and with the rich"'. The lower right hand panel showed the women at the empty tomb, with the text: 'He is not here, He is risen'.

Three centre panels portrayed 'our Lord rising from the Tomb as the Angels look on and the guards fall back' with the text: 'I am the Resurrection and the Life'.

The West Window

This was the great focal window at the west end of the church. Its inscription was: 'Dedicated by John Edward Cutler, of Valette, in this Parish, to the glory of God, as a memorial of many dear relations and friends, and a thank-offering for preservation during prolonged travel'. It depicted the 'single subject of the Adoration of Christ by the Shepherds and the wise men.... Angels look down on the Holy Family from the glass in the tracery.'

The smaller windows represented Resurrection scenes. To the left of the great central window, Mary in the Garden with three texts: 'Mary stood at the Sepulchre', 'Rabboni!' and 'I have seen the Lord'. On the right were three scenes; first, 'Thomas doubts no more' with text: 'My Lord and my God'; second, the disciples in the Upper Room with text: 'Peace be unto you', and third the charge to Peter by the lakeside, with the text: 'Feed my Lambs'. These smaller windows were dedicated: 'By public subscription to the glory of God, and in memory of Mary, wife of Henry Arnold Favell, M.A., Vicar of this Parish, and Canon of York, December 9th 1894'.

The North Transept

The dedication was: 'To the glory of God and in memory of Henry Arnold Favell, M.A., Archdeacon of Sheffield, Canon of York and 12½ years Vicar of this Parish, who died Sept, 21st, 1896'.

The large window was 'a fine composition centering round the figure of Christ the King, and illustrates the words of the age-old Christian hymn, "Te deum laudamus". In the tracery at the top of the window Angels sing the Tersanctus – Holy, Holy, Holy Lord God of Sabaoth, while below, surrounding the figure of Christ the King, Cherubim and Seraphim swell the chorus, playing on their instruments of music.' Below in four groups were the prophets, apostles, martyrs and saints.

In the east wall of the transept was 'a beautiful window of four small panels, representing the two sacrifices which sealed the Old and the New Covenants': Abraham with his son Isaac and Christ at Calvary. The dedication was: 'To the glory of God and in memory of Theophilus Marsh, born Dec. 10, 1826, died Nov. 21, 1881, and of Jane, his wife, born Jan. 13, 1831, died Jan 16, 1884. Erected by their children'.

The South Transept

The dedication was: 'To the glory of God and in memory of the Rev. William Milton, M.A., first vicar of Broomhall Parish, who died Sept. 26, 1884'.

The large window was 'composed of scenes from the life of our Lord', with a central panel showing his baptism and others depicting his parents, the wise men, Simeon with Jesus, and the presentation in the Temple. Lower panels illustrated Jesus blessing the children, with his disciples by the lakeside and with the woman of Samaria.

The window in the east wall, corresponding to the one in the north transept, was dedicated: 'To the glory of God and in memory of Arthur Thomas, Parish Warden of this Church, who died Nov. 25th, 1884. Erected by members of the congregation'. It had four panels: the upper two showed Christ teaching in the Temple, with the text: 'I was daily teaching in the Temple' and the Transfiguration, with the text: 'This is my beloved Son, hear Him'. The lower panels showed Moses giving the Law, illustrating the text: 'I will give Thee a law and a commandment' and Solomon building the temple, with the text: 'Solomon built the House of the Lord'.

North Aisle

The three windows in the North Aisle depicted the Miracles of Jesus.

The window nearest to the transept was dedicated: 'To the Glory of God, and in loving memory of Samuel Jackson, who died 28th January, 1890, and also of Eliza Jackson, his wife, by whom this window was dedicated, but who died before its completion – 22nd April, 1891'. Its three panels showed scenes from the raising of Lazarus, with the texts: 'Lord, if we sleep we shall do well', 'He that was dead came forth' and 'Lord, if Thou hadst been here my brother had not died'.

The central window showed the raising of Jairus's daughter, with three panels and three texts: 'Come down, and lay Thy hand upon her and she shall live', 'Damsel, I say unto thee arise', and 'Daughter, thy faith hath made thee whole; go in peace'. The dedication read: 'To the glory of God, and in loving memory of Henry Barker of Mexboro' House, near Rotherham, who died on the 9th March, 1876. Also of Sarah, his wife, of "The Rookery", Sheffield, who died on 13th April, 1891. This window is dedicated by their children'.

The remaining window was the most recent, erected: 'To the glory of God and in loving memory of Mary Anne Jowitt, who attended this church for over forty-five years and passed over on the 29th Dec., 1937'. It showed the raising of the widow's son at Nain, with the three texts: 'We went into a city called Nain', 'There was a dead man carried out', 'And he that was dead sat up, and began to speak'.

South Aisle

The three windows here depicted the parables.

The window nearest to the transept was dedicated: 'To the glory of God and in loving memory of Abram Brooksbank, J.P., of Southborne, Sheffield, born February 27th, 1822, died April 21st, 1890. Dedicated by his widow, Kate Mary Brooksbank'. Three panels depicted the parable of the talents, with the texts: 'Occupy till I come', 'Well done, good and faithful servant', 'Enter Thou into the joy of the Lord'. Below, illustrations of the Good Samaritan depicted: 'He had compassion on him', 'Set him on his own beast', 'And brought him to an inn'.

The central window was dedicated: 'To the glory of God and in loving memory of James Norton, Ashdell House, Broomhill, born March 13th, 1833, died July 21st, 1890, by his wife and children'. The left panel showed the labourers in the vineyard: 'The last shall be first and the first last'. In the centre, the Sower, and on the right, fishing: 'They gathered the good into vessels, but cast the bad away'.

The remaining window was: 'Dedicated by Kate Micklethwaite to the glory of God, and in loving memory of her husband, William Micklethwaite, born June 6th, 1841. Died March 24th 1887'. Its central panel showed the Good Shepherd, while the other two illustrated the texts: 'Ten virgins took their lamps and went forth to meet the bridegroom' and 'Five of them were wise and five were foolish'.

The Chapel

The side chapel was erected during the incumbency of Bishop Quirk. The east window, installed by the congregation in memory of its greatest benefactor, J.E. Cutler, depicted the meeting of Jesus with his disciples at Emmaus, with the texts: 'He took bread and blessed it' and 'Their eyes were opened and they knew Him'. The north wall window showed 'an Easter scene of Angels and Women at the Empty Tomb' and was dedicated: 'For a remembrance in the Lord of Harry Evelyn Marsh, who died January 10th, 1914: also of John Lockwood Marsh, Captain 1/4th Battn. York & Lancaster Regiment, who was killed in action, 16th Oct., 1915'.

APPENDIX 4

THOSE FROM THE CONGREGATION AND PARISH WHO DIED IN THE WORLD WARS

1914-18 WAR

Rowland William Bradbury
Arthur Edgar V Brightmore
Frederick Brocksopp
Archibald D Montague Brown
Edward F Montague Brown
Leonard Righton Burrows
Herbert Butcher
Basil Stuart Charles
William Arthur Colley
Henry Connelly
Alfred Mitchell Eadon
William Reginald Favell
Harry Garlick
Percy Green
Donald Henderson

Claude Edgar Hill
Leonard Barlow Hoyland
Clifford Hubbard
Henry Kelsey
Leslie Kirk
Joseph William Lownds
John Lockwood Marsh
Claude George Mawhood
Henry Middleton
Stewart Maleham
Stanley Cross Phillips
Arthur Plant
Douglas Parkin Raynor
John Watson Richardson
H.Gordon Righton

John Dawson Rodgers
Frank Rudd
Albert Smith
Ernest Spencer
Harry Storey
Edgar Taylor
Duncan W Thomas
Herbert Hugh Tomasson
Derwent C Turnbull
Ernest Edward Varley
Walter Tyrell Wall
Cyril Wheen
John Willey

1939-45 WAR

Graham Hardy Cotton
Geoffrey Alan Jonas
Robert William Jonas
Frederick Peter Marrian
Philip Lyon Marrian
John Edward Northend
C A Brian Slack
George Smith
Harry Stone
Albert Wells

APPENDIX 5

GEORGE PACE'S GROUND PLANS FOR THREE DESIGNS

1950 Plans (from the rebuilding appeal pamphlet)

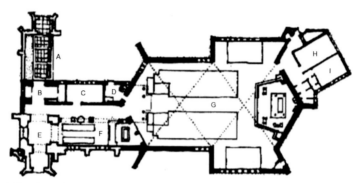

A: Existing North Porch, main entrance
B: Cloaks
C: Church Wardens' Room
D: Organ blower, etc.
E: Existing Tower and South Porch

F: Choir Vestry
G: Narthex
H: Stairs to organ and blower
I: Chapel
J: New Church

1955 Plans (digitally adjusted from architect's drawings)

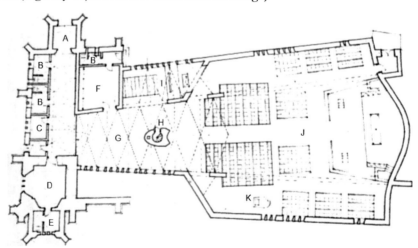

A: Existing North Porch, main entrance
B: Toilets
C: Church Wardens' Room
D: Clergy Vestry
E: Flowers and Cloaks [thru vestry]

F: Choir Vestry
G: Narthex
H: Stairs to organ and blower
I: Chapel
J: New Church

Final Plans (December 1960)

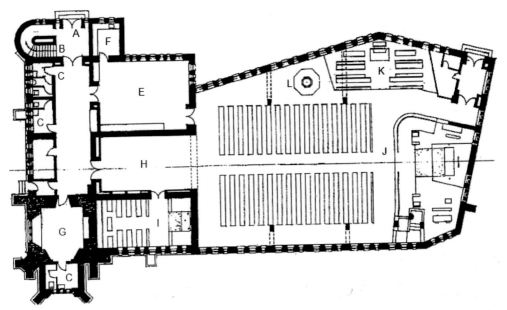

A: Main Entrance
B: Stairs to upper floor
C: Toilets
D: Church Wardens' Room
E: Choir Vestry
F: Flower Room

G: Priests' Vestry
H: Narthex
I: Chapel
J: New Church
K: Organ Console and Choir Stalls
L: Font

GLOSSARY – List of terms

Altar Frontal	A movable covering for the front of an altar
Apse	A semi-circular or many-sided recess, normally at the east end of a church
Aumbry	A recess in the wall of a church for sacramental vessels and sometimes for the reservation of the sacrament etc
Burgess	An inhabitant of a borough, possessing full municipal rights. See also 'The Sheffield Church Burgesses'
Buttress	A structure, normally of stone or brick, built against a wall to support it
Canon Residentiary	A member of the permanent salaried staff of a cathedral and responsible for the maintenance of its services, fabric etc
Church Army (CA)	An Anglican society of lay evangelists founded in 1882 by Wilson Carlile. Similar in some ways to the Salvation Army
Chancel	The part of a church containing the principal altar and particularly for the use of the clergy
Chapel of Ease	A building for the use of parishioners who live a long way from their parish church
Chartism	A political movement of the 1830s/1840s which demanded extensive political reform
Chasuble	The outermost liturgical vestment worn by clergy for the celebration of the Eucharist
Communion Table	The table used for the celebration of the Lord's Supper or Eucharist. A Protestant term
Compline	A late evening service at the end of the canonical day
Corona (pl Coronae)	A round pendant or hanging chandelier
Ecumenism	The movement in the Christian Church aiming to restore the unity of all Christian believers
Endowment	The property or funds devoted to the maintenance of an institution such as a church and to provide a stipend for the incumbent
Episcopate	The office or dignity of a bishop. The order or rank of bishops in the Church
Evangelical	In the Church of England, a member of the movement which lays special stress on conversion and salvation by faith in the atoning death of Christ. The movement originated in the 18th century to bring deeper reality into religion. In modern times divided between liberal and conservative wings
Lady Chapel	A chapel in a cathedral or church dedicated to the Blessed Virgin Mary, usually situated at the east end
Litany	A form of public prayer, usually consisting of a series of petitions
Matins	The order of public morning prayer in the Church of England. Originally one of the morning offices of the canonical day

Narthex	The western arm of a church, eastwards from the inner door
Paschal Candle	A large candle, blessed and lit at Eastertide
Perpetual Curate	The incumbent of a chapel or church of an ecclesiastical district forming part of an ancient parish. The office ceased to exist after 1969
Pew Rents	Payments for the use of a particular seat or seats in church. They were usually applied towards the clergyman's stipend and have now ceased to exist
Prebendary	A canon in a cathedral or collegiate church who receives the income of an endowment or prebend
Primus	The title of the presiding bishop in the Scottish Episcopal Church. He may be any one of the diocesan bishops
Reredos	An ornamental screen of stone or wood at the back of an altar and often decorated with figures or painting
Ritual/Ritualism	Terms used to describe the practices of those who, in the 19th century, wished to introduce medieval or modern Roman Catholic usages into the Church of England
Sedilia	Seats for priests on the south side of the high altar, generally of masonry
Sepulchre	A tomb or burial place, particularly applied to Our Lord's burial place in Jerusalem
Sitting	See 'Pew Rent'. Another name for a seat in church, in many cases paid for by the occupant
Stipend	The income of an office-holder such as a rector or a vicar
Succentor	A priest in a cathedral, generally the deputy of the precentor (who is responsible for the choral services)
Suffragan	A bishop appointed to assist the bishop of the diocese
The Sheffield Church Burgesses	A corporate body, chartered in 1554 to support the work of the parish church (now Sheffield Cathedral). In modern times active in religious and educational work and patrons of the living of St Mark's Church
Tower Louvres	An arrangement of overlapping boards or glass plates which admit air but exclude rain
Transept	The cross arms of a church, projecting at right angles to the main body of the nave and chancel

INDEX

Numbers in bold indicate the page numbers of illustrations.